Vaughn J. Featherstone
Elaine Cannon
Jack Weyland
George D. Durrant
JoAnn Ottley
Russell M. Nelson, M.D.
Lowell L. Bennion
Roy Darley
Connie Rector
Leonard J. Arrington
Karla Erickson
Crawford Gates
Emma Lou Thayne
Larry Chesley
Victor L. Brown, Jr.
George Romney
Linda Eyre

Bookcraft

SALT LAKE CITY, UTAH

Library of Congress Catalog Card Number: 81-69419
ISBN 0-88494-436-0

First Printing, 1981

Lithographed in the United States of America
PUBLISHERS PRESS
Salt Lake City, Utah

Contents

Vaughn J. Featherstone

I Knew It, and I Knew That He Knew It

In 1964, the company for which I worked asked me and my family to go to Los Angeles for a year to assist in an orderly turnover transition of a chain of fourteen stores our company had bought. My responsibility would be to head up all wholesale and retail produce operations. After we had arrived in California, I set about immersing myself in an orderly way into the operations so that I might be totally informed about every facet of my responsibility. I visited each store, introduced myself, and tried to put feelings of concern to rest. Several mornings I went to the Los Angeles produce terminals and accompanied our buyer. We usually started on the market between 1:00 and 2:00 A.M. I spent several days in the produce warehouse and met the personnel there, including the foreman, accountant, truck drivers, and other employees.

At two o'clock one morning I accompanied the produce buyer on the market. At five we went back to the warehouse to receive the produce we had bought. After assisting in loading half a dozen semitrailers with produce for our stores (about noon), I went to the retail operations. After visiting three stores, I was about ready to head for home. In the last store I received a phone call from the district manager who asked me to return to Downey, about a twenty-minute drive. When I arrived in Downey, the district manager was in his office talking to the produce buyer and the plant foreman of our wholesale operations. After inviting me in, the district manager said that these two men had come to him with an ultimatum: "Either you send Vaughn Featherstone back to Salt Lake City or both of us are leaving the employ of this company."

For those not acquainted with the Los Angeles market, let me explain that it takes five to eight years (most men claim) to be qualified as a buyer. The plant foreman was our back-up buyer. These two men had threatened to leave the company. A good buyer was worth his weight in gold and could make or break the wholesale produce operations of the company. Their threat was not to be taken lightly.

A decision was not made in haste or without involving the chairman of the board and the president of the company. Both of these top executives invited the two men to fly to the corporate headquarters to discuss the matter. They refused, saying, "You have heard our statement. Vaughn Featherstone goes or we go." The executives said they would fly to Salt Lake and meet these men part way. Still no deal. Finally they said, "If we fly down there, would it make any difference?" The produce buyer replied, "You have heard our conditions."

The company executives discussed this among themselves and attempted to come up with a reconciliation. After about two hours, during which time I was a silent observer, the district manager called me back into his office. He told me that Mr. Scott, the executive vice-president over all operations, wanted to talk to me. Mr. Scott said, "Vaughn, you have heard all the conditions. What do you think?"

After having pondered deeply, realizing the predicament the company was in, I said: "I like both men. They are both true professionals and they do their jobs well. As far as I am concerned, my family all live in Salt Lake and that is my home. I would prefer to live there. I didn't ask to be transferred down here; I came because the company felt it needed me. So, I would not feel one particle of remorse if I were sent home.

"On the other hand, the company is in a real predicament. Can we afford to have employees dictate the conditions of their employment and intimidate the company? I have never 'bought' on the Los Angeles market, but if you want, I will stay here and become the produce buyer and the plant foreman. I am indignant that these men feel they can dictate to this great company that I love. You make the decision, and I will support it either way."

He said, "Thank you for your input. We are going to stick with you." Needless to say, I wept and was humbled, but that was the beginning of long days.

The two men were put on the phone and Mr. Scott told them, "We want you to stay and we think you will be pleased with the benefits of this company, but it is your decision now because Vaughn Featherstone is staying."

They answered, "Fine. We are leaving as of tonight, and when the produce department managers hear we have resigned, half or more of them will also resign."

The executive vice-president still said, "Vaughn Featherstone stays." And the men left.

That night I went through all of our invoices to see what we bought and where. I memorized all of the prices. (I already knew "quality.") I got up at midnight and drove about forty-five minutes to the Los Angeles produce market, carrying with me the orders from all the stores so I knew our total buying needs. I went to each wholesale produce operation and explained what had happened, adding that I was the new buyer. I told them I had about twenty years in the produce business and knew quality produce. I told them that if they would be honest with me and deliver always what I had bought, I would continue to give them our business. I assured them that we would give them a fair price for high quality.

Then I told them that I was an honest man and they must never try to give me anything under the table: if they did, I would never buy another penny's worth of produce from them. At that time thousands and thousands of dollars were paid to buyers under the table. A deal would be made to pay twenty-five cents extra for a case of oranges and most of it would be given to the buyer. On a thousand cases of oranges you are talking about $250 under the table. I had heard of several buyers who were given gifts of new cars because of dishonest deals between buyer and seller.

It almost seemed to me that each supplier seemed relieved when I went through my little dialogue about honesty, ethics, and loyalty to good suppliers. By 5:00 A.M. I had bought everything we needed. I went back to the warehouse and started receiving the produce. It was just what I had ordered: no stove piping potatoes or good quality produce on the top of the box with poor quality underneath. Everything was high quality.

When the company truck drivers came that morning to load their trucks, they were shocked to see me there alone. I had observed each driver during the previous days, and so I invited the most personable and hardest working of them —a man with a good attitude—to be the plant foreman. He accepted and was delighted with the promotion.

I worked right with the men. We priced the merchandise and invoiced it and sent the trucks on their way at their normal time. There were no complaints about billing prices to the store, nor were there any complaints by the stores about quality.

Only one produce manager at retail level left the company when he heard the buyer and foreman had resigned. A slight adjustment (taking a second man and promoting him to department manager) solved that problem.

For the next three months, my schedule was something like this. I would get up at 11:30 P.M. or midnight and drive to the Los Angeles market. Between 1:00 and 5:00 A.M. I would buy, and then I would return to the warehouse. I would assist the plant foreman and train him until about 11:00 A.M. Then I would go out to our retail stores and work with and train people there between noon and 5:00 P.M. Finally, I would head for home. We would eat at about 6:00, and by 6:30 I was in bed. At 8:00 P.M. I would get up again and call all fourteen produce managers to get the orders from the stores. This usually took an hour and a half. Then I would go back to bed from 9:30 until 11:30 P.M. After a few weeks on this schedule, my personality changed. I was wearing pretty thin.

After about two and a half months of this, I went home one night and my wife said, "Dinner isn't ready. You and I are going to have a talk." I think my soul filled with self-pity. I was weary to exhaustion. If my wife didn't care about my sleep then neither did I. I felt like the Prophet Joseph: "If my life is of no use to my friends, it is of none to me."

We climbed into the car and drove to a large shopping center in Orange, California where we parked and sat in the car. In essence, she said: "Either you get this job under control so that you are not working these ridiculously long hours, or else. The children need you and I need you. We are away from home and we are all lonely. And, most serious of all, you are working yourself to death. The human body cannot take the kind of punishment you are giving it. Either you get your schedule back to a normal twelve-to-fourteen-hour day, or I will leave you."

It was the shock of my life. I said, "I will quit the company before I lose you and the children. My family and the Church are the most important things in this life to me. Please give me two more weeks to get my assistant buyer trained and then I promise you I will return to a reasonable schedule."

The next morning at about 1:00 A.M. I said to the assistant buyer, a wonderful Japanese man, "You will be the head buyer in the company two weeks from today."

He was terrified. He said, "It takes years to build a reputation and to be a professional buyer."

I said, "I know that. But it was turned over to me in one day, and if I could handle it in one day, you can do it in a total of about three months."

I went to the market with him every morning for the next two weeks, and then I turned the buying over to him. He became an outstanding, honest buyer.

When we were pretty well through the most serious problems, I was invited by the company to fly to the corporate offices and make a special presentation as to how the problems had been solved. Our sales were better than ever, our inventory was brought under control, the morale was high, the gross profit in each department had increased, and the quality of our produce departments had improved in both merchandise and better displaying. They asked me especially to focus on the things I had done during the "critical" period.

I prepared a presentation with overhead transparencies and reports from the operations. I outlined the problems and how we had solved them. But when I finished preparing my presentation, there was something missing. It took me a day or two before I could put my finger on it: I had not given credit to the Lord for solving the problem. I had spent many hours on my knees in prayer during that three-month period. So I went back and reviewed my presentation and inserted, near the end, "Tell them about prayer." After that had been done, my presentation felt complete.

I flew to Boise to make my presentation the next day. I went through it several times at the motel that night. Then I started thinking about the men who would be in the meeting. Most of them smoked and drank, and few of them were religious. I questioned whether talking about prayer in that setting was appropriate. After a great inner conflict, I knew that I must tell them about prayer. So I inserted in my outline above my prayer item, "Don't you have enough courage?" I was fearful that I might get involved in the presentation and, being with the executives, I might chicken out. This little insertion should shock me into not passing over it.

The next day in the meeting I was called upon to make my presentation. I shared with them the difficulties, the long hours, even my wife's threat to leave me. They hung with me throughout, and they had a good laugh when I told them about my wife. As I came near the end of my presentation and knew it had gone well, I nearly decided not to mention prayer. Then I looked down at my outline and read "Don't you have enough courage?"

It did what I had wanted it to do. I said, "I have given you a lot of mechanical and procedural tasks I did to work things out, but I am going to tell you now the only way I, or anyone else, could ever have solved the problems we had. It was through prayer. I spent more time on my knees seeking guidance than you would ever suppose. If it had not been for that help, I could not have done it."

It seemed to me that during that brief moment even the smoke stood still in the room. I had absolutely rapt attention.

I concluded my presentation and sat down. Later on, during the break, of the fifty men in the room only three said anything to me about my inclusion of prayer. One was a great member of the Church who said he was glad I had included it. Another was a very religious man who was a member of another church. He said how much courage it took to talk about prayer in front of the group. The third was a semi-active member of the Church who said he liked what I had said.

The important thing that happened was inside of me. I was grateful I had given God credit. There is no way I could have done it without him. He knew it, and I knew it, and now all of the top executives knew it. I felt totally at peace; I sensed I had done what God wanted me to do.

Before being called to serve in the First Quorum of the Seventy in 1976, Vaughn J. Featherstone was a counselor in the Presiding Bishopric. He has also served on the Church General Priesthood Committee, as a member of the YMMIA General Board, and as president of the San Antonio, Texas, Mission. He is a member of the National Advisory Council of the Boy Scouts of America and in 1976 received the Silver Antelope Award. He and his wife, Merlene Miner Featherstone, have six sons and one daughter.

Elaine Cannon

The Lord's Errand

Turning points can be a blessing. Often they come in life when a lesson is learned or a trial is tackled.

Turning points get a person going a different direction, feeling another way, changing a perspective.

When I was a young mother I was building my dream life. It was a dream life because it had little to do with reality. I dreamed that at least once a week children and mother were lovely-looking, charming, scintillating people seated around a bountiful and beautiful Sunday table with the handsome patriarch presiding in dignity and grace. That is how I dreamed the perfect life would be each Sunday. What went on during the week was another matter, but Sundays were supposed to be perfect.

Reality at that time was that we'd had a baby about every year, whether we needed one or not, until there was a houseful of little destroying angels who didn't understand my dream. There were five of them under seven, and their very young father was a bishop. He didn't understand my dream either. My husband did the best he could to juggle watching over his Church flock by day and night and especially on Sunday, and trying to be a father of his own brood whenever he could.

The real problem for me and my dream was that he was always late getting home on Sunday. I used to get very discouraged with the whole arrangement. Once I had a fever of 104 degrees and no husband to help me because he was visiting the sick. I recall wondering how sick one had to be to get the bishop to visit. Several times I considered making an appointment on Sunday to see this bishop, my husband.

There was one particular Sunday that was a turning point for me in that era of my life. The children and I came home from church to the table I'd set in its Sunday best the night before. The traditional Sunday dinner was ready and the little ones were anxious—but Daddy hadn't returned yet. We waited and waited and waited. Finally my dream was totally shattered by tired cries and hunger pains. I fed them little meals and helped them go down for their naps. Then I waited some more, becoming more frustrated, disillusioned, heartbroken, and furious by the moment. I worried some about why he hadn't called, but that didn't help. Pacing hadn't brought that bishop-husband-daddy home, and neither had children's tears nor my own angered spirit.

Then there came the turning point for me. I noticed my hunger. Hours had passed, and I hadn't eaten. I was certain my six-foot, six-inch partner in life had not eaten, either. I was reassured that he'd have come home to eat, if for no other reason, if he possibly could have! I prayed for his well-being, then ate, and settled down for a nap of my own.

I was awakened by his kiss. By then my spirit had sweetened and my attitude changed. I welcomed him warmly. I fussed over him and fed him and cupped my chin in my hands to watch him while he silently ate. When at last the meal was over, he turned to me and said seriously, "Elaine, before coming home today I had the most spiritual experience of my life as a bishop. A miracle happened, right while I was blessing someone. If you had spoiled it by sulking or scolding me when I showed up, I'd have been so disappointed I'd have had a hard time getting over it. Thank you for understanding. I've never loved you more."

I smiled and said nothing, but panic struck me inside— what if I had blown that? Inside I prayed my thanks to Heavenly Father that I got hungry and then smart enough to calm down and not be a spoiler.

It was a turning point. I turned away from selfish dreams to support my husband in his unselfish service to others. And I felt very good about it.

That was a beginning in a long life of coming to grips with priorities, of balancing along the fine line between good choices and better ones.

Another turning point came when I was in England on my first overseas assignment for the Church. I arrived late on Sunday at the mission home, and the flight had left its jet-lag mark. I was just changing my watch and my attitude to meet the local time and meeting schedule, when I suddenly realized that at that very moment the family I had so tenderly mothered would be going home from sacrament meeting—and this time the mother wouldn't be there!

A flood of homesickness swept over me, and I stretched across the guest bed in tears. I asked myself over and over again what I was doing so far away from my personal life and my loved ones.

A knock on my door and the alert that the wives of London's bobbies were waiting for me to speak to them startled me. I felt I had nothing to say, nothing to give. I wanted to be home. The trip had surely been a mistake.

Obligation pressed, however, and I dropped to my knees for help. As I poured out my heart and unhappiness, my need for the strength of the Lord to be with me, suddenly a new perception filled me. I was led to understand that I was on the Lord's errand and that I was to commit myself totally to the task at hand. My family would be all right.

The first turning point was to put my selfish dreams aside for the higher purpose of supporting my husband as he served the Lord. We were greatly blessed because of that. The second turning point was the knowledge that our children were Heavenly Father's, and if he needed some special help with others of his children, the family would be blessed while we met our commitments in the kingdom.

Line upon line the lessons come. Some are turning points, especially if the turning is in the direction the Lord would have us go.

Elaine A. Cannon is currently serving as the International President of the Young Women of The Church of Jesus Christ of Latter-day Saints. She is featured on the weekly radio program You and Your World *and has written many columns and books. She is a member of the executive board of the National Council of Women and is on the board of directors of the Promised Valley Playhouse, the Deseret Gymnasium, and the Lion House Social Center. She is married to D. James Cannon and they are the parents of six children.*

Jack Weyland

Possibilities and Promises

What is the probability that someone with a Ph.D. in physics, someone who dropped out of one course in creative writing because of poor work and who later signed up for a correspondence course in writing but never finished it, will someday write a first novel which will become a regional best-seller?

The probability is small but not zero—it happened to me.

I was born and raised in Montana. I graduated from Billings Senior High School and went to college at Montana State University in Bozeman, where I graduated in physics. Then I served a mission in New York and Pennsylvania.

After my mission I attended BYU as a graduate student in physics. (I enjoyed physics then and still do today. It is, after all, what I spend most of my time doing.)

One semester while at BYU I signed up for an elective course in creative writing. Within a few weeks it was apparent that I was in trouble—mainly because I didn't write very well. The one time I ventured to tell my instructor I wanted to write LDS fiction, he said, "You're not serious, are you?" Certainly a fair question, based on what he had seen of my writing.

I became discouraged and dropped the course and didn't think about writing again for several years.

Time passed. I married my wife, Sherry. We had a daughter Barbara, left BYU, and moved to South Dakota, where I work as a physics teacher at the South Dakota School of Mines and Technology. We gained more children (Dan, Brad, Jed, and Josie). We acquired a house complete with mortgage and lawn and garden and appliances which keep breaking down. We were given Church callings.

In the summer of 1971 I had the opportunity to work at BYU doing high-pressure research in the Physics Department.

While in Provo that summer, we had time to spare—no lawn to mow or water, no garden to tend, no Church callings, no appliances to fix, and no TV in our off-campus apartment. I decided to splurge and take a correspondence writing course from BYU. Especially I wanted it to be by correspondence. Never again would I tell anyone face to face that I wanted to write.

The course cost me, as I remember it, $37.50. In addition there was the typewriter to rent. Feeling guilty for spending money so lavishly, I decided to try to write a short story for the *New Era* magazine. Maybe they would accept it and send me money to cover my expenses for the course.

I wrote a story, and they accepted it. I wrote a second story and they accepted it. I wrote a third story and they rejected it.

That's it, I thought. *I'm through being a writer. It's a tough life.*

But the next summer found us at Oak Ridge, Tennessee, doing research—again with no lawn, no garden, and no Church callings. I wrote a fourth story and it was accepted.

Enough's enough, I thought. *Are you going to be a physicist or are you going to be a writer?*

There is a good chance I might never have written again except for one unforeseen event: I was called to be a bishop of our ward in Rapid City, South Dakota, the following December.

How, you ask, does that relate to writing?

In my job at the School of Mines, I am paid on a nine-month basis. At the end of every school year the problem becomes, *How do we survive this summer?* Previously we had left town to do research, but as a bishop that seemed impossible.

How else could I earn money?

I wrote Brian Kelly, editor of the *New Era*, and asked if I might submit more stories. He was very encouraging. So each summer for the next four years I wrote stories for the *New Era*.

Soon after I had been called as a bishop, our Young Women's president kindly explained that I was supposed to interview the youth once a year and talk about their personal goals.

A nice idea, I thought. *Youth should have goals.*

As the months rolled by and the youth of our ward came to my office, I learned much more about goal-setting. I became converted to it myself. I learned that goals should (1) be measurable, (2) be specific, and (3) have a definite deadline for achievement.

I became a goal fanatic. Anytime I was asked to speak in public it ended up being a lesson about goal-setting.

Never will I forget the time a young man, having heard me preach setting goals and achieving them, asked, "Bishop, when are you going to do something?"

A fair question.

After four years I was released as bishop, totally grateful

for the experience. I learned more about the Savior in those four years than at any other time in my life.

The next year I was asked to teach early-morning seminary. This meant getting up at five in the morning every school day in order to meet the class at six-thirty.

The following year I was called to be a stake clerk and didn't have to teach seminary, but since I was already in the habit of getting up early, I decided to continue getting up in order to write something other than stories for the *New Era*. (By this time they had a ten-year supply of my stories.)

For the next year I got up every morning and wrote. I wrote a screenplay and tried to sell it, but I was told that in order to sell a screenplay you need an agent. I tried to get an agent, but I was told that in order to get an agent you should have already sold some screenplays.

One January I went to New York City for a physics convention. While there, I saw a play by Neil Simon. *That doesn't look so hard*, I thought. So I wrote a play.

My play was rejected by some of the best play-writing contests in this country.

Screenplays didn't work, plays didn't work—maybe I should try a novel.

In May of 1979, I sat at my desk and wrote, "I will write a novel this summer and will send it to a publisher by October." A good goal—measurable, specific, and with a deadline.

That novel was *Charly*.

One more experience which is special to me. During 1978-79 I served as a stake clerk. In the spring of 1979 we learned that the first counselor in the stake presidency was moving.

Not only did I not aspire to the position, I prayed that Father would have the good sense not to call me to the position for the following reasons. First, we had only one car, yet our stake extended at that time two hundred miles to the west, two hundred miles to the east, seventy miles north, and sixty miles south. If I was in the stake presidency and traveling, my family would have no way to get to church. The only way I could then get a second car was to go into debt—and I knew Heavenly Father didn't want me to do that. Second, I didn't have any suits—they'd all been worn out being a bishop. All I had was one ratty sport coat which was certainly adequate for a stake clerk. (I'm sure you're sizing up my degree of spiritual maturity by the fact that I felt a suit was necessary. Okay, so I'm not a spiritual giant.)

In my prayers I had presented a solid case. There was no way I would be called.

A few weeks later my brother-in-law called long distance and, out of the blue, said he had been shopping for clothes a few days earlier and found a suit he really liked, but it was the wrong size. He said he had bought it anyway and was sending it to me.

Mere coincidence, I thought.

Next, my mother-in-law—not a member of the Church —called us and said, "There're too many cars in our driveway. Do you want one?"

She paid our way to Boston for a summer vacation. We flew out and I drove the gift car home. (I went home early to write *Charly* while my wife and family stayed on an extra two weeks.)

In the course of the next few weeks I inherited two brand-new Johnny Carson suits, six white shirts, some ties and some socks—all nearly new, all close to my size.

Finally, when our stake president extended a call to me to serve in the stake presidency, what could I say but yes? I'd seen it coming for weeks.

I am the person who can sit in a class and never say much of anything. Sometimes in a new place, it's easy to imagine I am invisible, so little impression do I make on people.

How is it, then, when I'm traveling down the interstate in Utah on my way to an autograph party, to hear on the car radio, ". . . Now from the pen of Jack Weyland . . ."

It's nice. I like it.

But the questions that come back again and again are these. What if I had turned down the call to serve as a bishop? Where would I have learned what I needed to know about goal-setting? What if I had not accepted the call to teach early-morning seminary? Would I ever have decided to get up at five every morning to write without that year's seminary experience? (No way!)

My experience has taught me this: When we accept a call, we often think how much of a sacrifice it's going to be and how noble we are to sacrifice our time and talents, and maybe how much in debt to us Heavenly Father is going to become.

But when we serve him, there is no sacrifice. He blesses us well beyond what we deserve, and when we finish we are more in debt to him than ever before.

I love the opportunity to tell the world in my writing that what we have is the gospel of Jesus Christ.

He blesses us richly for any service we give. He helps us discover talents we never knew existed within us.

Now, what about you?

A native of Butte, Montana, Jack Weyland is known for his many short stories and his books. He is the author of the books Charly, Sam, *and* First Day of Forever and Other Stories for LDS Youth. *He is an associate professor of physics at the South Dakota School of Mines and Technology in Rapid City, South Dakota, and writes a science question-and-answer column for a local newspaper. He and his wife, Sheryl Raner Weyland, are the parents of five children.*

George D. Durrant

A Season
for Changing

In my late teen years I learned that just as there are changing seasons, there are also seasons for changing. The soil of my soul had been fertile in my childhood, but during my late youth it became a bit rocky. The hot sun of peer-group pressure and my own adolescent uncertainties had stunted my personal and spiritual growth.

But then, just as warmth follows winter, the conditions for change gently settled into my soul as subtly as the beginnings of spring.

As a plow cuts through the hardened ground, so had my feelings been harrowed up by the cutting blades of discouragement — discouragement caused by my being in college physically but not mentally and of being in, but not fully involved in, the Church.

This most paralyzing of all opposition seemed to create the dark clouds which tumbled and boiled in my mind and made it so very hard to see. But it was these dark forms which contained the gentle raindrops that moistened my inward desires and made me want to grow. Prayerful moments caused the clouds to part and I sensed a sunshine coming from far beyond where I could see.

The gentle rain of inspiration was falling. The "bottom lands" of my heart were warm and fertile. The condition of light was right. All that was needed was for a loving, caring sower to come forth to sow.

And a sower did come forth, and then another, and still another.

The first to come was my mother.

"Don't quit college," she said gently.

"Why should I keep going? I'm not doing well."

"Because what you are supposed to do you must go to school to do."

"But, Mom, what am I supposed to do?"

"I don't know, Son, but you must go to school to do it."

"I'm quitting," I said, with less conviction.

Tears filled her eyes. I held her close and after some seconds backed away to arm's length and replied with a gentle smile, "I was just kidding." I hadn't been kidding. But somehow the seed she had sown was already beginning to find root. I kept going to school and made it, so that I could do what I was "supposed to do."

The second sower to come forth was the Master Sower himself—the Holy Spirit.

It was just after Christmas and only a few days since my mother had persuaded me to return to school. I went to get my grades from the fall quarter. I had to grasp them quickly because a fellow behind me was trying to see them and they were not in an envelope. I stuffed the thin paper into my pocket without looking at the dismal details. I walked across the campus to a place where I knew I could be alone. I mustered my courage and pulled my grades from my pocket and looked at them. As I did so, I heard an inward voice. It was that wonderful, still, small voice that sows so many seeds. To me it said as I looked at my grades, "George, you can do better than that."

I crumpled the paper in my clenched hand and stuffed it back into my pocket. I turned and walked across the campus to the library. It was a most pleasant place. I was sorry that I had scarcely ever thought to go there before.

As the days passed, I bought the books the teachers expected me to buy. I left my traditional seat on the back row and went down front. I purchased a pad of paper and a pen. Everything the teacher said, I wrote down. I read the books, I passed the tests. My grades became acceptable. The Holy Spirit had sowed the magnificent seed which had convinced me: "George, you can do better than that."

This same sower visited me again a few days later when, in response to an invitation, I attended a party which turned out to be less than it should have been. Smoke filled the room; and, although I wasn't participating in any of the inappropriate behavior, I was there. Once again, as I sat looking about, I heard the voice within my soul. This time it said, "George, you don't belong here." I excused myself and never went back.

The third sower was from among the Lord's anointed.

He came during my season for changing. Just a few weeks had passed since I had first felt the thrill of inward growth. I was sitting in a devotional at Brigham Young University when this man arose to speak. He spoke of miracles. He blended the serious and the sacred with the humorous and the inspiring.

I fought my emotions because I didn't want to cry. I laughed with moistened eyes. He took my emotions from one edge of my heart to the other. He talked of laying hands on the sick and seeing them become well through the holy priesthood. He talked of the faith of the Maoris in New Zealand. He spoke of one among them who had died and was brought back to life through the administration of the elders. He talked of a boy who had polio. He described how he and a young bishop had laid their hands on this young man and he had become well. When he finished speaking, I didn't want to leave. I felt at peace. He had sowed a seed in my heart that caused me to feel with all deep conviction, *I want to be good. I want to serve. I want to love the Lord with all my heart and soul.*

This sower's name was Matthew Cowley. If the increase from all the seeds he sowed were ever gathered together, it would be a mighty store.

The clouds of winter had parted and had given way to spring. The sun shone brightly in my heart. This had indeed been a season for changing, and I was experiencing new life.

Just as there are changing seasons, there are seasons for changing. And when those seasons come and the proper sowers come forth, there grows within our souls a harvest of limitless joy. And so it was for me.

George D. Durrant received his B.S., M.S., and Ed. D. degrees from Brigham Young University. Before serving in his current position as the Director of Priesthood Genealogy, he was a teacher of religion at BYU, a seminary teacher, and principal of the Indian School in Brigham City, Utah. He has written hundreds of filmstrips used in the Indian seminary program and has been instrumental in writing Family Home Evening manuals as well as several books, including Love at Home, Starring Father, The Art of Raising Parents, Someone Special, Starring Youth, Fun and Names, *and* Get Ready, Get Called, Go. *From 1972 to 1975 he served as president of the Kentucky-Tennessee Mission. He is married to Marilyn Burnham Durrant and they have eight children.*

JoAnn Ottley

The Apples in a Seed

The world is full of thrill-seekers, and to one degree or another each of us is among them. It must be profoundly exhilarating to conquer a mountain, run a white river, or race a car at breakneck speed; and the thrills must go far beyond the physical. As a matter of fact, there must be something akin to that type of thrill in stepping out on a stage, facing a hungry audience, and conquering a performance of excruciatingly difficult music waiting to be brought to life. That one I knew about.

It is my strong contention, however, that there is an infinitely higher thrill which, like climbing a mountain or singing a beautiful song, once experienced never stops begging to be repeated. That thrill has its beginning in the private and personal discovery of revealed truth—the universal laws by which God is governed and by which he governs. It has its development in private and personal decisions to test that law through acts of faith followed by effort. And the consummation of that thrill comes in watching and, indeed, experiencing in body and soul the miraculous unfolding of events as they proceed by methods far beyond our feeble capacities even to dream of.

Those discoveries began in earnest for us midway through my husband's work toward his master's degree in music. Without saying too much about sacred things, it should be noted that there had been profound new spiritual insights and guidance along the way concerning his pursuit of higher degrees and that there began to be impressions and events gather to propel us toward a study program abroad. Now, for some people that wouldn't sound like such a big deal. For us it was a big deal. We were already past thirty and had a seven-year-old son, a house full of belongings, no particular yearning for such an adventure, certainly no funds after so many years in school and, to be honest, a large amount of "scared stiff." But the feelings were there to be acknowledged: they didn't go away no matter how hard we tried, and we knew that, no matter what, our desires to be used by the Lord as he wished would have to come first, beyond comfort and even beyond "scared."

It is important to this story, too, in trying to paint a personal viewpoint and testimony concerning the immensity and superiority of God's ways, to note that much of my twelve years of marriage had been spent weeping and begging the Lord for children. After the first five years, many expensive and painful tests, and a special blessing, we welcomed our beautiful baby boy. Then the next seven years were spent pleading for a brother or sister (and frequent pointed reminders to the Lord that my patriarchal blessing referred to "child*ren*") until finally, following a heartbreaking miscarriage, I learned my lesson and promised the Lord I would never beg him again, that we would submit ourselves to his ways and his timetable. The infinite peace which followed could never be described and has remained. It was an important chapter in our book of learning.

We applied, with the help of wonderful friends and advisors, for Fulbright Study grants. Weeks later, when informed that we had been awarded dual grants for study in Cologne, West Germany, it was relief, joy, discomfort, sorrow, fear and giddiness, all rolled together.

Moving is one thing, but total dissolution of a household is a horse of a different color. Every rubber band, fruit jar, paper clip and stocking, as well as furniture and appliances, had to be dealt with, decided upon, and disposed of—give away, stow away, throw away, or take—and since we could take only a steamer trunk and three suitcases with which to set up housekeeping for a year, that was a job similar in size to chopping down a forest.

The ocean voyage was a dream come true for all three of us and a high adventure for our starry-eyed little boy. The docking on a sunny day in north Germany was too beautiful to be true, and we were as starry-eyed as he was. From there, however, the stars rapidly gave way to the realities.

How does one paint a picture of bittersweet? Any description less than extreme in either direction does not do it justice. It was a year of feeling strange, of often being badly treated, of never-ending rain and grayness. (We three made a pact that we would never again willfully purchase any object of a gray color after living in a gray apartment on a gray street surrounded by gray skies.) It was a time of not being needed, of being unable to say deep and complex things because of insufficiency in the language, of concerns for our son, and of great boredom since school responsibilities were not great enough to occupy much time. (How many people do you know who have played Monopoly all the way through to the end?) We were used to having no money, but having lots of time and no money is a miserable combination.

The arrival of the postman and of dinner time, were the great high points of most days, even though the meal was most often only soup. The apartment was in the industrial section of the city and had a kitchen which measured fifty-three by sixty-two inches. For a daring young single student that's not much of anything, but for a thirty-two-year-old American housewife spoiled by such luxurious conveniences as a kitchen range, it's an adjustment. But I became very proficient at putting on a fried chicken dinner for the missionaries and ourselves by juggling pans in tandem on our double hot-plate. There were some culinary disasters, but we had a lot of laughs. It was necessary for me to do the laundry by hand, and as I bent over the bathtub, scrubbing with all my might, I would vow: "My Grandma did it, and I can do it!"

There were extreme challenges at school, too, especially at the beginning. They included writing down all the words I didn't understand from one dear professor, who spoke like greased lightning and had a lisp, so I could go home and look them up and try to figure out what he had taught me. I'll always remember studying Italian in a German textbook, and lying on the floor in a body motion class keeping one eye open (eyes were supposed to be closed—I don't remember why) so I could copy the others' motions because I couldn't understand the teacher's dialectic German. Then there was the professor who gave my husband a tongue-lashing in front of his class one day for having his hands in his pockets.

The bitter side was tough, and there was little between the bitter and the sweet. But the sweet was immense—excursions out into the magnificent German countryside, Christmas in the Black Forest, trips to castles to view true antiquity, the overwhelming kindness of the German Saints and of many at the school, marketing at the fresh-air market each week, the joyous opportunity of having young missionaries frequently in our home, new foods, togetherness, and appreciation for home. Our experiences as Latter-day Saints were glorious as we attended meetings and conferences and responded to invitations to sing throughout the area. We attended operas and concerts performed at a level we had not experienced before and were bathed in a whole new professional level of awareness. So much learning. Our year taught us worlds in a professional sense, but much more in terms of life perspective. It broadened our horizons in every sense and provided a kind of learning in which we have come to believe deeply, though it doesn't come cheap. Price tag, again.

There is truth in the idea that man is a product of his decisions. That being the case, the big turns which occur in a life most often have their beginnings in decision-making processes, some large and some small, some which produce miniscule changes and some which are virtually endless in their effects on that life. It seems also that the difficulty of a decision proves to be in direct relation to the immensity of its after-effects, placing its discomfort level somewhere near childbirth. Such was the case as we approached the end of our year in Germany. It became apparent that we had a heavy decision to make: whether to remain in Germany to work professionally or to return home. There was every reason to believe that I could have an immense career if we decided to pursue it.

We were on the Lord's errand, however. We knew it, and we knew that such a decision had to come from him in order for it to be forever effective. Turning points are usually excruciating, and even more so when one is concerned with something beyond his own desires. We fasted many times and prayed incessantly. We wrote home to family and professional friends for advice. We counseled together endlessly. We were miserable. As we came to the point of total frustration, my good husband asked that I make a written personal expression of my viewpoint about the whole situation. I saved that letter as part of my personal history, and it is, in part, as follows:

"1. Not only my first inclination, but my first duty, is that of wife and mother. Idealistically I should be able to say that being a professional singer does not necessarily get in the way of being a wife and mother, but even here and now, where there is less pressure on me professionally than I have had for years, I find myself constantly facing the choice: 'Shall I study, sing, memorize, or shall I spend time with my son or mend my husband's coat?' Yes, perhaps I should be capable of doing both things *totally*. I don't honestly know whether I am.

"2. I have apparently been given a rare gift by the Lord, and I want with all my heart to serve him with it. Teaching alone does not serve the Lord with the gift of singing. And yet, try as I may, I cannot find more than the slightest spark of desire to pursue an operatic career, even for a year. I have prayed fervently for the Lord to give me that desire if I am to do so in his interests, but I have found, at best, only a sacrificial willingness to 'endure' such a pursuit. I wonder if one *can* succeed in something he only endures.

"3. If we do not stay, we will be going against almost every piece of advice we have been given by those whom we love and trust and admire. It will be necessary to be very sure of that decision in order to have their support in what we do and in order to be at peace with ourselves in the years to come. 'We shall not pass again this way.' "

The preparations for the turn were agonizing, but through a series of steps, each important, we arrived at the turning point. It came at a precise moment—not to one, but to both of us—appropriately enough during a sacrament meeting. It was concise and complete: Our work was not in Germany, but at home.

No one could understand our decision. We also couldn't precisely understand, but we didn't need to. We were at peace with the decision and ever so happy to be headed home.

Since this is a first-person account, and I have of course told it from my own perspective, I feel that it is very important to explain that this intense and invaluable training ground which we walked was territory into which we were thrust for the purpose of preparing: first for preparing my husband for the immense calling he would later receive, and second for preparing us as a team to fulfill a particular little corner in the work of the kingdom at this time, including my work as a professional singer. Whatever else has come of it is frosting on the cake.

The chapters go on, year after year, of course, but just two need to be mentioned. As we made preparations to leave Germany I became very ill. It was hard to function in all the things which had to be done, both at school and at home. Finally, on the day before our departure, I went to a physician, praying all the way I had chosen someone who could understand my German description of my symptoms. He did. He spoke flawless English so my poor German didn't matter. The verdict: impending motherhood. Words could never express it. It was as though the Lord had said, "You have done as I asked; now I will do as you asked." The three of us laughed and cried together. It was a moment of unbelievable sweetness. Allison arrived eight months later. What joy!

The other vital chapter came considerably later (though there were important ones in between) when the call came from President N. Eldon Tanner's office that he wished to see my husband. The rest is history. To be conductor of the Mormon Tabernacle Choir is at once a great honor and a great consuming responsibility, one which he not only would never have sought but would vigorously have resisted except for his total commitment to serve how and when and where the Lord wishes him to serve.

Thrills? Yes. And adventure and drama and all that goes with those things. The supreme thrills come coursing through the soul as the mortal and the celestial merge, as we see how high are God's ways compared to our own and how much greater are his designs for us than our own.

"Anyone can count the seeds in an apple, but only God can count the apples in a seed."

Soprano JoAnn South Ottley studied music at the University of Utah, Brigham Young University, and the Staatlische Hochschule fur Musik in Cologne, West Germany. She has been a soloist with major United States symphony orchestras, Ballet West, the Utah Opera Company, and the Mormon Tabernacle Choir. She also is the vocal coach for the Choir, is the spiritual living leader in her ward, and has performed and spoken at many women's conferences. She is married to Dr. Jerold D. Ottley, conductor of the Tabernacle Choir, and they have two children.

Russell M. Nelson, M.D.

A Mighty Change

In September 1949, as a young surgeon in training, I gained the opportunity to work in the surgical research laboratory of Dr. Clarence Dennis at the University of Minnesota in Minneapolis. He had received a grant to explore the possibilities of creating an artificial heart-lung machine. Such a device was deemed theoretically to have possible value to assist, at least temporarily, the patient with failure of the natural heart or lungs.

I had just turned twenty-five years old and was still green and enthusiastic enough not to know that the task couldn't be done. Eagerly I joined Dr. Dennis and his colleagues, only to find that the "simple" task of making a machine that could pump and aerate the blood, even for a brief period of time, was overwhelmingly complex.

The details of the scientific trials and triumphs are not central to the theme of this story, but success ultimately followed. The first use of a heart-lung machine for open heart surgery came in March 1951, in Minneapolis, using our creation, thereby opening a new era of investigation, innovation, and eventual application to hundreds of thousands of patients then unknown to us.

But in the process of this endeavor, a mighty change in my own sense of comprehension occurred. Prior to this, I had not concerned myself much with the miracle of our own endowment of the physical body we possess. But as our intense, detailed study of one small part of the body was challenged by the goal of trying to create something that would duplicate its function, I was humbled. I was humbled not only with my own sense of insignificance and relative ignorance, but with an overpowering conviction that God is our Creator, so omniscient and beneficent.

How we struggled to create valves to control the direction of blood through the artificial heart! Then I looked at natural human heart valves with a new sense of wonder. Four tiny valves open and close over a hundred thousand times a day, over thirty-six million times a year, serving without our awareness or gratitude. They are soft and billowy as a parachute, yet tough as sinew. To this date, man has not been able to create such a material, one that can fold and unfold that frequently without stress-fatigue and ultimate fracture.

The heart each day pumps enough blood to fill a two-thousand-gallon tank car, and it performs work equivalent to lifting a 150-pound person to the top of the Empire State Building, while consuming only about four watts of energy, less than the dimmest light bulb in our home.

At the crest of the heart is an electrical transmitting center that sends signals down special lines that cause millions of muscle fibers to beat together with a synchronized response that would be the envy of any conductor of a symphony orchestra.

The machine we made occupied many square feet of space. The pump our Creator made occupies a space about the size of one's fist, and it doesn't even need to be "plugged in" for power. Its power is provided not by battery or by cord, not by compressed air or by nuclear energy, but by a process known only to God. With this realization, I began to fathom the real meaning of the scriptural passage I had previously glossed over: "For the *power* is in them" (D&C 58:28, italics added).

The period of my mighty change then extended well beyond my focus on the heart. I began to meditate about our other gifts, just as intricate and amazing. The human brain with its countless combination of power cells and of recording, memory, storage and retrieval systems serves as the headquarters for the personality and character of man. The capacity of the brain seems to be infinite. The more it is stimulated and challenged, the more it can do. Wise men can become wiser; experience builds preparation for more experience; greater exercise of intellect brings forth increased intellectual capacity.

Indeed, each time I marvel at the work a modern computer can do, I reverently respect, even more, the mind of man that developed the computer. The more I respect the mind of man, the more I adore and worship the God who created man's mind.

In my awareness and amazement for the major miracles represented by the human heart and brain, I sensed I may have been like the spectator at the football game dazzled by the brilliance of the passer and the pass receiver, while overlooking the essential and often unheralded participation of the blockers and linemen.

Then I gave thought to those mechanisms within the body that regulate and control thousands of variables without our conscious knowledge. We are aware of the thermostatic system that regulates our body temperature. In a like fashion, there are mechanisms to control the amount of water we retain and to govern the blood levels of important constituents such as sugar, salt, protein, minerals, and vitamins. When the intake of needed elements is low, these items are conserved. When the intake is high, excesses are eliminated. All this is done to maintain homeostasis and balance in the marvelous chemistry of the body.

Even more astounding is the ability of the body to adapt. I consider the many climatic and dietary differences of our Father's children who dwell in the Arctic Circle . . . compared with those who live in Polynesia, for example. Much of the Eskimo's diet is made up of fat, which is acceptable and even necessary to sustain life in this very cold climate. The Polynesian, on the other hand, eats a diet provided by his environment. All work and thrive on the unique intake divinely provided for them.

As I watched some three-year-old children playing one day, I saw them drinking water as it ran down the sidewalk from a neighbor's garden. I suppose the germs they ingested were incalculable, but not one became ill. As soon as that dirty drink reached their stomachs, hydrochloric acid there went to work to purify the water and protect the lives of those children of God.

While considering protective mechanisms, I realized that one of the most marvelous is the skin, the most rugged yet senstitive cover one could imagine. If I were to create an "artificial skin" could I conjure a cloak that would at once protect from and yet perceive and warn against injuries that excessive heat or cold might cause? We could, if we had to, get along without our arms, legs, eyes, or ears; we could possibly even survive with somebody else's heart or kidneys. But without this cloak in which we all find ourselves, our skin, we would die. If a large enough portion of his skin is destroyed, man cannot live. Encasing all other vital parts, the skin, the largest human organ, serves as a barometer to emotional as well as physical needs. When another part of the body is ailing, the skin can reflect it by flushing and sweating. When one is embarrassed, the skin blushes. When one is frightened, the skin pales. All of this is programmed into this sensitive organ by a beneficent, wise Creator who knew and perfectly understood all of our needs from the beginning.

Another protective mechanism is that of pain, not only from the body cover but in the delicate sensory areas of the mouth. Warnings are received from the mouth that guard the delicate and yet relatively insensitive esophagus that would be burned if we swallowed drinks that were too hot.

Think of the protection afforded in the circulation of blood. It carries self-sealing properties that come to the rescue in the event of injury and possible leakage from that system.

Consider the fact that broken bones heal.

Consider the ability of the body to manufacture antibodies and concentrate bacteria-combating forces in zones of infection. All are essential to survival.

Then I glanced at the heart-lung machine in the laboratory, the object of our creation. Could it heal a cut or seal a leak? Absolutely not! Each leak caused spraying and spillage that meant hours of clean-up time tacked onto the end of the day.

The ability of the body to repair itself is so remarkable that a countless number of home remedies receive favor essentially because of that power of healing. Previously in the care of wounds, I had used this preparation or that, this bandage or that, uncritically and ungratefully oblivious to the fact that God would heal the wound almost regardless of what I would do, as long as I kept it clean and gave him the chance. Now, I give him the credit too.

Now I realize that the ultimate decision a physician must make is whether the process afflicting the patient is one that will improve with the passage of time or one that will get worse. The former needs only supportive care, while the latter requires more aggressive intervention to convert it (we hope) to the kind of process that *will* improve with time.

If I could create anything that could heal itself, that would be a miracle. But could that be done, would that self-repair process then be limited so that self-healing would not be perpetual and infinite? This question brought me to an even greater sense of our divine creation. At the same time we have been given the power to heal, we have been given the process of aging, by which we are guaranteed a limit to self-healing and to the length of life as we now know it here upon the earth. My Creator is my Father. He wants me to have this experience here on earth, but he wants me to return to him—and the process by which that is ensured is also built in. What a staggering realization that is to me!

One of the main purposes in our receiving bodies is that we might have families. The two tiny cells that unite in the process of reproduction to form an embryo contain all the information and potential to develop each organ system that functions and to create tissue that will differentiate to form the eyes that see, the ears that hear, and the fingers that feel the wonderous things about us.

All of this causes me to look at man as God's greatest creation.

Amazing as the body is, capable of so many miraculous functions, the most humbling perception in my mighty change was the realization that the body of man is *not* the *object* of God's creation, but that it serves only to be incidental to something transcendently greater: the *spirit of man.*

The body serves the spirit. It is the mortal tabernacle for the spirit. The purpose of the body is to house the spirit so it may gain the experiences provided by life on earth. The great accomplishments in life are not physical, but spiritual. Life is given that we may develop faith, virtue, knowledge, temperance, patience, brotherly kindness, godliness, charity, humility, and diligence.

The gifts of the spirit, such as righteous power, compassionate service, and love, have little to do with the physical aspects or bodily functions of man.

God has ordained that we use our divinely created *bodies* to enable us to attain *spiritual* growth and development. So to me, it is pure sacrilege to let anything penetrate the body that might be harmful. To me, it is irreverent to let the gaze of precious eyesight or the sensors of touch and sound supply the brain with memories that are unclean. To me, it is a sign of faithlessness if one feels a need to add unprescribed drugs, preparations, or products to "add" to the power of the body to function optimally.

"Men are, that they might have joy," said Lehi (2 Nephi 2:25), and joy comes from using the precious body the Lord gave us for the divine purposes that he intended.

Some individuals have conjectured that there is a conflict between science and religion. For me, the scientific challenge of attempting to duplicate even the smallest part of the function of one organ system evoked a mighty change in religious awareness. The mighty change occurred in me; I now had the vision and the maturity to see the truth that had been there all along: that God is my Creator and my loving Father. Gratefully I acknowledge my absolute awe, faith, and eternal love for him.

Dr. Russell M. Nelson practices medicine in Salt Lake City, Utah, specializing in cardiovascular and thoracic surgery. He is a staff surgeon at LDS Hospital, where he also serves as vice-chairman on the hospital's board of governors. He served as the General President of the Sunday School for the Church from 1971 to 1979 and is now a Regional Representative. He and his wife, Dantzel White Nelson, are the parents of ten children.

Lowell L. Bennion

From the "Golden Days" of My Youth

When I was a boy of fourteen, I went to work on a ranch in isolated country 180 miles from my home in Salt Lake City. In those days, this was a long way away. In the valley where the ranch was located, there were only three families and a few hired men and boys.

One day my boss sent me into the mountains with a hired man to change the course of a mountain creek. Much of the water which came to us through the old channel sank into the sand before it reached the ranch. A new canal had been made. Our job was to connect the mountain stream with the new canal. It was an exciting job and took nearly a week to accomplish.

My pardner, in charge of our two-man crew, was a fine fellow and a skillful, steady worker. He had one bad habit. He was a chain smoker. He didn't offer me any cigarettes, but I must confess his smoking was mighty interesting as we sat around the fire in the early darkness.

On the third day at camp, my pardner ran out of tobacco. His Prince Albert can was empty. I watched this good man become nervous, restless, and irritable. He searched the ground around the camp, picking up cigarette butts out of the dirt where men and horses had walked. The nearest store was miles away, and we had only a wagon and team for transportation.

Watching my good friend's misery and helplessness, I vowed then and there that I would never be a slave to a "weed" or drug.

A few years later I was serving a mission in Bielefeld, Germany. Near Bielefeld was an institution for the mentally ill and retarded, called Bethel. Over five thousand mentally handicapped people in all stages of their limitation resided there. In addition, there were wonderfully devoted ministers, doctors, nurses, and others who cared for them. Bethel was a little city all by itself.

One day we missionaries toured the little city and found out that it had been established by religious people who had compassion for the ill. We asked about the cause of their illness. The guide said that it was believed that heavy drinking of alcoholic beverages was one important cause.

There are many causes of mental illness and mental retardation; and heavy use of alcohol, we have learned in recent years, is one of them but only one.

A few days after the visit to Bethel, my companion and I were tracting in a nearby village. We knocked on a farmhouse door and were invited in by a rough growl-like greeting.

In the corner of the room was a half-drunken father. Hearing our message, he ordered us to get out of the house "with our _____ _____ _____ Mormonism." As we left, two forlorn-looking sons about our age waved good-bye to us.

This was the second time in my life when I was deeply moved to thank God for my Mormon upbringing and for my father and mother who had given me a healthy mind and body.

My wife and I studied at the University of Vienna following my mission. This was during the Depression in 1931-1932. We lived on sixty dollars a month of borrowed money. We had no telephone, no car; we bought no clothes, and we walked or rode the streetcar everywhere we went. Saturday evenings we went to the grand opera house and sat in the top gallery for twenty-five cents each. Sometimes I stood up for fifteen cents.

The end of the month found us often very low on cash. We usually went to the market—which was held in a nearby street—to buy vegetables, fruit, and meat from farmers. Our object was to make a soup to last us until our monthly check would arrive.

One day after we had spent our last pennies on food at the market, as we were leaving I stooped down and picked up some outer cabbage leaves one of the farmers had thrown away. This embarrassed my good wife and she chided me good-naturedly. I told her that a new flavor in the soup the third day might taste pretty good. As we got near to the street where we lived, we heard a young man about my age singing a heartrending song in the street.

> My mother loves me not
> My father I do not know
> I do not wish to die
> I am so young. *

A few people would open their windows and toss small coins to him in the street. I noticed that he not only picked

---

*In German: Meine Mutter liebt mich nicht
                   Meinen Vater kenne ich nicht
                   Sterben will ich nicht
                   Bin doch so jung.

up the coins but also gleaned cigarette stubs and cigar butts from between the cobblestones where men and horses walked. I turned to Sister Bennion and said, "In our poverty I may have to pick up cabbage leaves to feed my hunger, but thanks to Mormonism, I don't have to pick up cigarettes and cigars from the dirty street."

In the years which have followed these experiences of my youth, I have learned that there are things in life and religion that are far more important than not smoking and not drinking. Humility, honesty, chastity, faith, love of God, and love of neighbor are the great fundamentals of religion and of life.

I have also learned that many fine people have developed smoking and drinking habits. I do not judge or condemn them. (Many would quit if they believed they could.)

But I shall be eternally grateful to my religion for giving me the incentive to leave tobacco, liquor, and other harmful drugs alone. (I have enough faults without them.) I have also come to appreciate the words of Alma to his son, Shiblon: ". . . see that ye bridle all your passions, that ye may be filled with love" (Alma 38:12).

Lowell L. Bennion received his bachelor's degree from the University of Utah and his doctorate from the University of Strasbourg in France. For 26 years he was the director of the LDS Institute of Religion at the University of Utah. He has been professor of sociology and the associate dean of students at the University of Utah. As a writer, he has numerous manuals, lessons, and books to his credit including Jesus the Master Teacher, Understanding the Scriptures, *and* The Things That Matter Most. *He is currently the Executive Director of the Community Services Council in Salt Lake City. He married Merle Colton and they have five children.*

Roy Darley

A Crossroad
in My Life

I have been an organist in the Salt Lake Tabernacle since 1947. As I look back, it occurs to me that much of what has taken place in my career and in my personal life has resulted directly from one crucial decision I had to make. If I had hesitated or wavered at that crossroad, or if I had not taken the initiative to press for what I earnestly desired, I am sure things would have turned out very differently for me.

This turning point came at the conclusion of my mission in the eastern states in 1943. Shortly before my return home, I learned that the organist at the Washington, D.C., chapel was leaving his position. This meant that there was an opening for a new organist, who would also serve as director of the Bureau of Information at the Washington chapel. I journeyed to Washington to look over the facilities. The position was attractive, but I knew that with World War II raging, there was virtually no possibility that I could be chosen to fill the vacancy.

En route home by train, I decided to stop off in Toronto, Canada, and see my dear friend, President Joseph Quinney, who had been president of the Logan Temple near my home town of Wellsville in Cache Valley, Utah, and who had been my father's mission president in Canada. He was now serving a second term as president of the Canadian Mission. I stayed with him for about two days, at the end of which time he and two missionaries took me down to the train station. About a hundred feet from the door of the train, President Quinney collapsed. We picked him up and carried him over to a bench. He was still conscious and assured me that he would be all right, urging me not to delay my departure for Salt Lake. Reluctantly, I boarded the train.

When I reached Salt Lake, I felt that I should report the incident in Toronto to President David O. McKay, who was then second counselor to President Heber J. Grant and in charge of the missionary work for the Church. So I phoned Brother Joseph Anderson, secretary for the First Presidency, and succeeded in getting an appointment with President McKay. President McKay was grateful to be informed about President Quinney, since he had not reported the problem of his poor health to the First Presidency. (President Quinney died two weeks later in another Canadian train station.) I took the opportunity at that time also to report my mission.

Concluding my report, I remarked, "President McKay, I would like to go on a second mission for the Church." This took him by surprise; apparently very few twenty-four-year-old missionaries just home from the field had reported directly to a member of the First Presidency, let alone requested a second mission to follow immediately. He asked me just what I had in mind, and I told him that I had heard about the post in Washington and would like to be considered for the appointment. He quickly replied that they already had someone in mind and were merely waiting for his draft board to release him so that he could start his assignment. I suppose I could have let the matter drop there, but I had the gumption to add, "If by some chance his draft board will not release him, would you consider me for the appointment?" Again President McKay appeared surprised, but after a brief pause he gave me a faint smile and answered "Yes."

The law at that time required a missionary to report to his draft board within ten days after his return home. I did not want to go home until I heard whether the other candidate's draft board would give him a favorable response, but I also wanted to stay within the law. So instead of returning directly to Cache Valley where my draft board was located, I stayed with close friends—Brother and Sister Charles R. Snelgrove—in Salt Lake. Word finally came that the draft board would not release the other person.

I went back for a second conference with President McKay. He told me that if my draft board would release me, the Church would issue the call to me. That seemed a simple enough request. I returned to Cache Valley, reported to my draft board, and there discussed the possibility of a deferment. They instructed me to meet with Colonel H. Arnold Rich, who directed all of the Utah draft boards. It was a very brief encounter. With all the authority a colonel could muster, he pounded his fist on the desk and told me in no uncertain terms that I was going into the army. He even put that directive in writing and sent it to my draft board.

But, feeling that Colonel Rich had far overstepped the bounds of his authority, the local draft board determined to run its own operation, whereupon there followed several communications between the board and President McKay's office. A resulting divergence of opinion created a stalemate: President McKay wanted the local draft board to defer me, after which the Church would call me; the draft board wanted the Church to call me, after which they would defer me.

Feeling somewhat frustrated but not knowing what to do about it, I was having lunch with my parents at our home in Wellsville one Sunday after Sunday School. It had been a good day. As we sat there chatting about the routine events of the morning, suddenly it came to me that I must go to Salt Lake the next day. With a sense of urgency and without even waiting to finish lunch, I went to the phone and called Brother Allen over in Hyrum (he ran a milk truck to Salt Lake City every day except Sunday) to arrange for him to pick me up as he passed through Wellsville the next morning. Hitchhiking was a must during the war because gasoline was rationed and traveling by private car was severely restricted.

As I walked into the office of the First Presidency about nine o'clock that Monday, Brother Anderson greeted me in surprise and said, "Brother Darley, I don't know what brings you down today, but I am certainly glad to see you. President McKay is leaving tomorrow morning for Old Mexico and will be gone a month. He has to come back to his office sometime today, so if you want to see him, I suggest you remain here until he returns."

I waited from 9:00 A.M. until 4:00 P.M., not moving from my chair the entire time. Finally President McKay came in. He greeted me and told me he could spend only a brief minute with me. When we sat down in his office, he began by saying, "Brother Darley, I can't call you to this position." He put his hand on a stack of papers on his desk and continued. "These papers are all requests for deferment. I can't issue your call until after your draft board has deferred you." He told me he would turn all the correspondence over to Brother Franklin Murdock. Then he shook my hand and was gone. Disheartened, I returned to Wellsville.

The next day Brother Murdock, who was in charge of all travel for the Church, began studying the stack of letters President McKay had left for him, and when he came across the two counter-proposals concerning me, he took the information to President J. Reuben Clark, who read over the letters. President Clark's action was simple and decisive: "Call this brother down and we will set him apart."

Had I waited that Sunday in Wellsville to think over the situation for twenty-four hours, I would never have been called to Washington. Had I not gone to Washington, I would not have gained the valuable experience of recital work there. Had I not gone to Washington, I would not have met Lieutenant (j.g.) Kathleen Latham, who was stationed in the nation's capital and teaching Relief Society at the Washington chapel and who became my wife. Had I not gone to Washington, I probably would not be an organist at the Salt Lake Tabernacle today.

Organist Roy M. Darley has played at the Salt Lake Mormon Tabernacle since 1947 and has given about 5,700 recitals there. When he was 25 years old he was called to be director of the Church Bureau of Information in Washington, D.C., where he also did recital work. In 1961 he was given a special assignment by the Church to be the organist at the Hyde Park Chapel, London, England. While there he was awarded his Associate from the Royal College of Music. He is currently a Tabernacle Organist assigned to play with the Mormon Youth Symphony and Chorus, and periodically he is the organist for the Mormon Tabernacle Choir. He and his wife, Kathleen Latham Darley, have five children.

Connie Rector

A Growing Commitment

The story of my conversion to the Church begins with my conversion to Hartman Rector, for it hinged on a decision we made together when we were young, long before we ever heard of The Church of Jesus Christ of Latter-day Saints.

Hartman and I had dated occasionally over the course of about three years. World War II had just ended, he was in the navy, and through our letters we had gained a certain understanding of and confidence in each other. When he came home on leave, I was ready to give him my full time and attention, and that was our real beginning. We spent the short time we had together in talking of how we intended to spend the rest of our lives.

He took me to visit his parents' farm. We walked and talked, climbed over fences, and sat to rest under a giant old elm tree whose roots were partially exposed above ground.

The roots became convenient seats for us as we sat facing each other, holding hands.

Hartman then told me that he felt we were each put here on earth for a purpose, not merely to stumble around until we die and fall to the earth and rot. To believe that that was all there is to life seemed senseless to him. He intended to find out the truth about life and whether there is a life after death. He said also that he did not understand why Christ had to be crucified and how what he did could be efficacious in our own lives, but that he intended to gain an understanding of it. He invited me to search for truth with him and *never cease to grow* in understanding. There beneath the elm tree we pledged our love for each other and our determination to grow together.

"Never cease to grow" became the slogan of our commitment, and that commitment grew in the months that followed—months mostly of letters and partly of Hartman's leaves—until Hartman could come home from the navy for good.

We were married shortly after he came home, and we settled down to the business of farming. I was less than helpful for I knew next to nothing about running a farm home, garden and livestock.

We were very busy during those days, up at 4:30 A.M. working briskly all day long, but we did find a little time to read the Bible regularly together and to wonder about many things. The local country preacher came out and rode on the tractor with Hartman, yelling above the engine's roar his argument on some of the questions Hartman put to him. He would have liked Hartman to join his church, but Hartman was not interested in joining. Instead he continued pleading in his prayers the same supplication he had made all of his youth: "Dear God, please lead me to the truth, *please send me* the truth!" It seemed strange to me that he was praying that God *do* this for him. How could God *bring* truth to someone? His attitude puzzled me, but I loved him for it.

Before long it became apparent that because of a skin cancer on his lip, Hartman could not work outdoors in the sunlight all day—we would have to give up farming. He changed jobs, and we moved to Kansas where our second child was born and where we continued to pursue religion, joining the congregation of a dynamic and popular preacher, and—typically—asking questions all along.

It was not long before Hartman was recalled into the navy because of the Korean conflict, and soon we were on our way to San Diego, where he would be assigned to a squadron and a carrier. We found a house to rent there and visited with Hartman's two married sisters, but he shipped out for three months in Hawaii a few days before our furniture arrived from the midwest. When the van line finally unloaded our belongings, I began unpacking and trying to settle myself and the children.

The next morning the doorbell rang and I made my way around and over packing boxes to get to the door. There stood two young men, impeccable in dark suits. They explained that they were from The Church of Jesus Christ of Latter-day Saints and were taking a religious poll in the neighborhood. Would I mind answering a few questions?

It was amazing to me that a number of the questions on that poll were very similar to the ones we ourselves had pondered, such as: Is God's church on earth today? Do people today need a prophet of God? Did we live before we were born on this earth? Is there a life after death? The young men marked something after each of my sage replies and said they would call again. They claimed that the doctrine of the church they represented answered all these questions. Imagine that! If only Hartman were there to talk to them. I would have to try to remember all the things Hartman and I wanted to know and see what this church professed about those matters.

In a few days the two young men were back at the door —Elder Raban and Elder Flygare. (Funny that they should both have the same unusual first name!) I supposed they would tell me the results of their poll, but instead they told me that they had a message which would give the answers to the questions and they would like the opportunity to present the first part of that message to me today. They asked me if I knew any Mormons and said that was what they were. I thought they had previously said that they were from some *other* church! However, they did look legitimate and harmless enough to give them a chance to at least present their story, so I let them in. Hartman and I had always been ready to talk to anyone who was willing to discuss religion. So few people were.

The missionaries gave me a Book of Mormon and I became intrigued with it. I loved their lesson on the Americas before Columbus and the Book of Mormon. Pieces of a giant puzzle began to slide into place.

The elders continued with the lessons, almost weekly. I read the assignments in the Book of Mormon and felt that it was quite possibly true. Wouldn't it be wonderful if it were true—the truth Hartman had been praying for! After all, he had prayed, "Please send me the truth." Could it be that these missionaries had been *sent?*

I tried to explain their message to Hartman in letters, but each time I knew that my words were miserably inadequate; and I was afraid he might stop the elders from coming, before he really considered their message, so I did not write much about it. It was such a *fantastic* story, and sometimes I wondered how I could possibly be believing it (but it all really *did* make sense!).

The elders taught me how to pray. Actually I had never *really* prayed before, and now that I wanted to know if what I was studying was true, it was really quite reassuring—as they suggested—not to take *their* word for it but to ask God about it.

Prior to Hartman's homecoming, the elders and I fasted for forty-eight hours. I heard him as he arrived unexpectedly in the middle of the night, he and another officer friend who had transported Hartman and his paraphernalia from the airport.

The first thing he asked me when he walked in the door was, "Now, what is this about Joseph Smith?" I was still half asleep. This was exactly what I had been afraid of—that I

would not be able to do justice to the true story of the
Prophet and how he translated the Book of Mormon plates
and restored the true Church of Jesus Christ.

I tried to explain it to Hartman, just what I'd been studying (in a nutshell)—how it answered this question and that
question and it all sounded right to *me*.

He looked at me as if he'd never seen me before and told
me that this story was *incredible!* "How *could* you believe
such a fantastic tale?" he asked.

This was like a nightmare. I could not answer another
question. I sank into a chair and cried uncontrollably. I
blurted out that he had been gone three months; that I had
been so anxious for him to get home so that I could tell him
that here were the answers to all his questions, or so it
seemed to me; that here I had thought I was going to hand
him, on a silver platter, what he'd been praying for! "And
now you won't even give it a chance!" I ended. Oh, this was
awful!

"Well," Hartman said, "if it means *that* much to you, I'll
at least read what they left you." And he picked up the Book
of Mormon and walked into another room with it, leaving
me astonished but grateful.

He began reading the book. He believed it with all his
heart, and from that time on he took the lead in our
complete study of the teachings of the Church, its history,
and its leaders. We had very little time to study together,
however, because he soon went overseas.

At that time it was customary to teach an investigator
many lessons before baptizing him. Since Hartman would be
gone about nine months this time, we decided to wait until
he returned and be baptized together. In the meantime we
planned to continue studying and to write to one another
about our progress.

My mother came to stay with me as long as she could to
help me with the children while Hartman was away. I had
always had a very close relationship with my mother, yet I
recognized that she took an extremely negative view of life
and that this disposition had alienated her from virtually

everyone but me. For all her negativism, though, I had not expected the reaction she showed to my studying "Mormonism." Everything I had learned about the Church was beneficial, and I told her so, but she nevertheless ranted wildly about immorality and polygamy and heresy and proselyting people from other churches. I hardly knew what she was talking about, but now I really dug in and researched and studied all I could, until I could understand the reasons behind her insinuations and accusations. Through all this I had a testimony that the doctrines of the Church were true and that the Book of Mormon was inspired scripture, just as much as the Bible. I knew that Joseph Smith was really a prophet and I believed that David O. McKay was now the Lord's prophet on earth.

I loved everything I was reading about the gospel. It was all very thrilling to me. In fact, I could think of little else but the inspired doctrine in the standard works of the Church. I felt aloof from worldly cares; as I performed my tasks, my heart was singing. I had a new love for nature and for all of humanity and a deep-down appreciation for my darling little children. From now on I wanted to be the very best in everything that I was capable of, and I was convinced that God would expand my capabilities. I felt so grateful!

In February Hartman wrote to me that since every day he was at war he ran the risk of being killed, he thought it best not to postpone our baptisms any longer. He'd have liked it if we could join the Church together, he said, but at the time it just didn't seem wise to wait. I agreed with him, and plans were made.

Since my mother did not want me to join the Church, there would have been no point in telling her the date set for my baptism. It was something I had to do, for myself, for my husband, for our children, and for all of our future posterity, but I was very, very sad that night. Of all the people I cared about, Hartman was the only one who agreed and approved, and I adored him for his acceptance and his complete love for me and the Lord. But at that moment he was so far away in Japan!

I had found this scripture through study and it was not only my comfort but also my compass.

> Whosoever therefore shall confess me before men, him will I confess also before my Father which is in heaven.
>
> For I am come to set a man at variance against his father, and the daughter against her mother, and the daughter in law against her mother in law.
>
> And a man's foes shall be they of his own household.
>
> He that loveth father or mother more than me is not worthy of me: and he that loveth son or daughter more than me is not worthy of me.
>
> And he that taketh not his cross, and followeth after me, is not worthy of me. (Matthew 10:32, 35-38.)

I knew what these passages meant. And they gave me the strength I needed. In addition, Hartman had written to me saying he would be baptized in Japan by McDonald B. Johnson, a young LDS sailor aboard ship, whom he admired very much.

Hartman and I went to our stake patriarch for our patriarchal blessings after being in the Church for one year. Among many other things he told us, he said in Hartman's blessing, "*You will never cease to grow* in the work of the Lord." Our slogan which we had adopted as kids.

When those who had time after time borne testimony to me laid their hands upon my head and confirmed me a member of the Church, I had a strong reaffirmation throughout my whole being that the Church was true and that the ordinance being performed was efficacious. Though I was calm and at peace, there was a burning in my chest and tears of joy ran freely from my eyes. I knew again that I was doing the right thing. The sweetness and light that I had known from time to time as I studied, I experienced once again. I have never been sorry for our decision.

Since Connie Daniel Rector joined the Church she has been a ward YWMIA president, a member of a stake Sunday School board, and a member of a stake Relief Society presidency. She is currently attending BYU to work on her degree in English and is a ward Relief Society president. She has co-compiled five books, including the No More Strangers *series. She is married to Hartman Rector, Jr., of the First Quorum of the Seventy. They are the parents of nine children.*

Leonard J. Arrington

The Prayer
for a Miracle

In the fall of 1956 my wife, Grace, and I took our children to Pasadena, California, where I would spend a year as a Visiting Fellow at the Henry E. Huntington Library and Art Gallery in nearby San Marino. Further south and west, in Los Angeles County, lived Elmer and LeRuth Tyau. Elmer had been a student of mine at Utah State University, and LeRuth was a favorite cousin. Before graduating from USU, Elmer and LeRuth had decided to move to southern California. There they were married, and Elmer obtained employment as a chemical laboratory technician with AeroJet Corporation in Azusa, California. Our family visited with them shortly after arriving in southern California.

One afternoon (January 28, 1957) while I was working at the library, the library assistant came to tell me that I had an urgent telephone call. LeRuth was on the line, and she frantically said there had been an explosion at the laboratory

where Elmer worked. He had been severely hurt, and the
doctors did not expect him to live. But he must live! "You
must hurry over and administer to him!"

Fortunately I had taken the car that day. I do not now
recall why I had driven; almost always I took the bus. I
phoned Grace to inform her and then drove as quickly as
possible to the AeroJet plant. Under normal circumstances
the drive would have required an hour, but I'm afraid I did
not pay much attention to the speed rules and arrived in
forty-five minutes. LeRuth was there waiting for me.

As I entered the room where Elmer had been placed, it
appeared that the doctors held little hope for his survival.
With LeRuth kneeling beside me, I hurriedly anointed him
and offered a prayer.

"Our Heavenly Father, in the name of Jesus Christ and by
the authority of the Holy Priesthood, I pray . . ."

LeRuth: "Yes, Heavenly Father, bless him, bless him to
stay alive."

"Having faith we pray . . ."

LeRuth: "Yes, we have faith, Heavenly Father. He must
live!"

Our prayers went on—earnestly, tearfully, fervently.
Here was a brother whose whole side had been severely
damaged by a powerful explosion. So torn apart was his
body that his intestines had been wrapped in a towel as he
was rushed to the hospital. Doctors had told LeRuth that he
would surely die quickly. She must get "their priest" to
perform "last rites."

A miracle must happen. But we had faith that it would,
and said so in our prayers.

We had an inner confirmation that Heavenly Father
recognized the genuineness of our faith. The blood technician who came to check Elmer's blood type also had a special
feeling as he saw that the patient was a former fellow student
and Church member. And the elder from the local ward
assigned to assist with the administration had lived in the
same dormitory with Elmer. The doctors spliced Elmer's
vital organs together, and they were blessed with the skill to

save his life. Miraculously Elmer survived; doctors made extensive skin grafts and performed other operations to "fix him up." Our prayers were answered.

After five years, during which time Elmer completed his schooling at USU, Elmer and LeRuth moved to Hawaii, Elmer's birthplace. He had been fitted with an artificial arm, and his body was healed so that he could live a normal life. Tall, strong, and handsome like his Hawaiian mother and athletic like his Chinese father, he could even run and swim. He soon pursued a career as a counselor in a Hawaiian rehabilitation program.

Now, twenty-five years later, Elmer and LeRuth have a family of seven children, all of whom are valiant in the kingdom. The three sons have filled honorable missions— one in Taiwan, one in Hong Kong, and one in California. All of the children are talented, active, and beautiful.

LeRuth and Elmer have engaged in intensive genealogical research on the Tyau family and have done temple work for twenty generations of Tyaus, back to A.D. 1300.

The priesthood administration and the prayers of the pleading wife and mother were heard and answered affirmatively by our Heavenly Father.

Leonard James Arrington was born in Twin Falls, Idaho. He is married to Grace Fort Arrington and they have three children. He received a Bachelor of Arts degree from the University of Idaho and a Ph. D. from the University of North Carolina. He has been a professor of economics at Utah State University, and he served for many years as Historian for The Church of Jesus Christ of Latter-day Saints and is now the Brigham Young University Lemuel Redd Professor of Western History. He has written many books on economics and history, including Great Basin Kingdom *and (with Davis Bitton)* The Mormon Experience.

Karla Erickson

A Lucky Lesson for Life

When I was just a young girl, full of dreams and hopes for my life, my ultimate dream was to own a horse. I lay awake nights fantasizing rides across our open land and I grew intense with the desire to have that dream come true.

One afternoon my father took me to a neighbor's farm where, in the pasture, stood a reddish-brown Arabian mare. She had three white-stocking feet and a bald face, but what I noticed the most were her big brown eyes. Dad sensed that I wanted her more than anything else in the world, and he saddled her for me to ride to our farm which was several miles away. As I rode her for the first time, it was just like a storybook dream come true, and I was on my way to living happily ever after. However, even though I was old enough to enter college the following autumn, I still had not experienced enough of life to realize that often when dreams come true, there is not a guarantee that the joy will last forever.

Since I felt that I was the luckiest person alive, I named my horse Lucky. She was an interesting horse to get to know. First of all, she was very high-strung, and trying to catch her to ride was a job in itself. But once she was caught and saddled, what great times we shared! She possessed inexhaustible energy, and she loved to run. Often we rode through open fields where there were only a few rattlesnakes, rock chucks, field mice, Lucky and me. The love I felt for her seemed to enhance the love I felt for the land, and as she ran I silently thanked my Father in Heaven for letting me be alive to experience those moments.

But there was also another side to owning Lucky. She did not like being confined, and many times when I went to catch her the pen was empty. One morning my dad received a phone call from an irate neighbor who asked if we owned an Arabian horse with three stocking feet. She was in his potato field causing havoc with his crop. For as many times as she brought me sheer joy, there was an equal number of times when she caused me to get angry or upset. But the moments of joy always took precedence and I never regretted owning her.

In fact, I found myself relating to her in many ways. My energy level was also high, and I often felt as though I wanted to run faster and faster. I despised the night as a robber of my time because I was made to go to bed and rest. I also cherished my freedom and rebelled when I was made to feel trapped—much as Lucky must have felt when surrounded by a fence.

Lucky was teaching me lessons about life which no one else had been able to teach through words. One lesson I'll always remember had its beginning one late summer afternoon. We had been out for several hours, and as we turned to head for her pasture she started to run full steam. My heart raced with excitement! Just as I spotted our trailer in the distance, Lucky's foot fell into a chuckhole and she stumbled. I sailed through the air and landed on my back on the hard dirt clods. When I came to my senses I was crying, and my first thought was that I would probably die right then and there. My whole body ached. I didn't know if I even wanted to try to pull myself up off the ground. Though my vision was blurred with tears, I turned my head to see two big brown eyes gazing at me, and for the first time I noted concern and warmth in Lucky's eyes.

I hurt too badly to try and swing up onto her bare-back, but I managed to walk slowly to the trailer and Lucky followed obediently. It seemed I had used every ounce of strength I could muster to get there.

Several years passed. College came and soon I had graduated. New dreams emerged and my life was full when I met Barry, who would become my husband. Oh, how I dreamed of our raising a little boy and girl together! Barry and I were ecstatic when we learned after several years of marriage that we would be parents for the second time. Our little son was fourteen months old when his sister was born six and a half weeks prematurely with hyaline membrane. When our pediatrician told us that our newborn daughter would probably not live longer than seventy-two hours, I reexperienced the intense desire to have my dream come true, just as when I had dreamed of owning a horse. But this time it seemed that too many odds were stacked against me.

Upon the doctor's suggestion, Barry called his father and our bishop so that our little girl might be given a name and a father's blessing. In that blessing he expressed to our Father in Heaven our desires to raise our little girl here on earth, and he pledged that we as parents would do our best to help her become all she was capable of being. Ten days later we carried our new daughter into our home and introduced her to her big brother. Truly, my dream had come true and the tears could not be restrained as we expressed our heartfelt thanks to our Father in Heaven.

Even though she had to be fed every three hours around the clock, I found it a joy to get up with my baby daughter through the nights and try to get her to take some nourishment. She was so weak that often she took forty-five minutes to an hour to drink only a quarter ounce of formula. My opportunities for rest were rare.

After several weeks of the routine of caring for our young son and daughter, my physical strength waned. One evening Barry had gone to play Church basketball and I had just finished feeding Cori when I heard the door close softly. I thought that Barry was going to try to lift my sagging spirits by scaring me, but when I saw him stumble into our bedroom, I knew that he was not playing a joke. He had torn his Achilles tendon, and the next day he was in a cast.

I was devastated! Barry was the only one who had been able to help me get through the days and nights, and now, now he needed *me* to help him. I fell on my bed and started to sob. This time I had been thrown so hard on the dirt clods of reality that I doubted if I ever wanted to get up. Then I felt a soft pat on my back. I turned around to see the big blue eyes of our little boy, and they were full of the same warmth and concern which I had seen that one afternoon in Lucky's big brown eyes. His blue eyes seemed to carry the same message as her brown eyes had done: "I know you are hurt and ready to give up, but come on—I know you can pull yourself up if you will only try."

Now, many years later and after many more dreams come true, I still cling to the memory of that one afternoon when Lucky threw me on the hard dirt clods. At every stage in my life there have been dreams which kept me wanting to move ahead. And yet, the moments of picking myself up off the ground are the ones which have provided true joy, the moments when I still feel like the luckiest person in the whole world.

Karla Carlson Erickson was born and raised in Shelley, Idaho. She graduated from Utah State University with a degree in English and has taught English literature and become a free-lance writer. Her published works include Take Time to Smell the Dandelions, Kids in the Kitchen, *and* Invest in the Best—Your Kids. *She has served as an advisor in the Young Women's program of the Church and as a ward Primary president, and she is currently a cultural arts specialist. She has lectured before many church and civic groups. She and her husband Barry have five children.*

Crawford Gates

Decisions, Decisions

One of the most important decisions of my life came during the summer of 1940 at Hermit's Canyon Camp west of Stanford University in California. The rolling, oak-laden foothills, now overrun with research laboratories and expensive residences, were then open, empty, and somehow mysterious. That summer was my second as director of a Boy Scout camp in Hermit's Canyon. I had completed two years of college, one at College of Pacific in Stockton and the other at San Jose State College. My bishop in the Palo Alto Ward felt that, in spite of my age (I was eighteen and a half), he should recommend me for a mission call, and while planning for an early fall departure I spent many a night pondering the implications of the seeming-eternity which a two-year mission suggested to me.

On a typical night I would complete the campfire program, make my rounds to see that the Scouts were properly bedded down, then climb to the water tower hill overlooking the camp, and on an old dented bugle do my best with "Taps." The sound floated out over the dark valley below, sometimes echoing back when the wind was right. Then I would proceed to walk in darkness or moonlight through the deep grass under the dappled shadows of the oaks, thinking, praying, trying to find the answers that the questions in my heart called for.

What questions? Some were universal, some immediate: Is there really a God listening to my queries? If he creates and governs a galaxy that holds two hundred billion stars and a million galaxies beyond that, what interest could he possibly have in my small concerns? And what of Christ? Is he real? Are the scriptural accounts valid? Did he really rise from the tomb and live, and does he really guide a church on the earth today? How can his death on the cross possibly have anything to do with me or my life? And is his will really manifest through the high-pitched voice of Heber J. Grant? Is it true that he wants me to go on a mission?

And what about Joseph Smith? Does his account of the words of Jesus in the Sacred Grove ring true? Do these words have substance? important substance? profound substance? Could I with conviction declare Joseph as a true prophet of Jesus Christ? What is the essence of this thing called priesthood? And what does "restored" really mean? The questions came in a flood, and some of them returned night after night like an itch that couldn't be scratched.

I had some immediate concerns beyond these more general but fundamental ones. I had the opportunity for a music scholarship my junior year at College of Pacific. Some nonmember friends pointed out that this scholarship likely would not be available to me two years hence, and wasn't it somewhat foolish to forego such an immediate opportunity for the unpromising activity of a mission? Then there was the prospect of loss of all the social delights that I enjoyed in rich abundance: dances, dates, pretty girls, parties, football games, and movies. These were not the fare of the dedicated and committed missionary. What desolation to lose these for the long double-year stretch! And for what purpose, for what other rewards I was not sure.

Of the questions prospective missionaries ask themselves I suspect few escaped me. On those rolling hills surrounding Hermit's Canyon Camp I wrestled with my angel for a number of weeks when the pressure of work relaxed temporarily.

At that time, while I had read the New Testament and the early pages of the Book of Mormon, I had no real knowledge of the Doctrine and Covenants and could not then have referred to the ninth section which I later came to know, love, and use. But inadvertently I employed a principle of decision-making taught via this section. I did not leave it entirely up to the Lord to give me the answer to my questions. I studied them out in my own mind. I tried to imagine what might happen to me if I turned down the mission call. That proposition conjured up another host of unpleasant visions and ideas. I studied the alternatives carefully, exploring them in my imagination, projecting myself on each course to see what might happen should I elect to do this or that.

I don't remember that my answers came in any blinding flash of light. But I do remember quite clearly that before the summer was over, I came off those Hermit's Canyon hills with a conviction to go on that mission and to serve the Lord well and with all my heart. My bosom burned within me and I knew my decision was right. This was the fundamental answer. All the other answers would find their place in due time—if not now, then later.

I knew the Creator of those vast galaxies was my Father, and that he was concerned with the decision-making process at Hermit's Canyon in the summer of 1940. He walked with me, but he let me retain my freedom to make my own choice. I knew that Jesus had really come forth from the tomb; I knew that his suffering in Gethsemane and on the cross would pay the price of my shortcomings if I would repent of them, and that it had opened the door to eternal life. In my heart of hearts the words of Joseph rang true to me wherein he said, "I had seen a vision; I knew it, and I knew that God knew it, and I could not deny it." Neither could *I* deny it, Brother Joseph. The same Jesus who gave you commission in the Sacred Grove caused my heart to burn within me so I was certain that that commission was true . . . and that it is important! And wonderful!

So I reported to my bishop that I was ready and anxious to go. The recommendation went in, and the prophet of the Lord called me to the Eastern States Mission, where I labored with all my heart. Not that I was the perfect missionary; I was not. Nor was I very successful by the usual standards. But I endeavored to give a good gift to the Lord with what limited ability I had, and the Lord blessed me—and has blessed me to this day in innumerable ways.

The Hermit's Canyon decision process is the pattern of the Lord as taught in the Doctrine and Covenants, even though I did not know its source at the time. I studied my problem out thoroughly, then I asked the Lord, and he confirmed my direction, causing my bosom to burn within me. In a world of indecision and conflicting directions, I am thankful to the Lord for this wonderful principle. It operates on the basis of righteous laws which come from Jesus Christ. What a wondrous blessing it is to be able to make an important decision and thereupon to receive confirmation of its wise direction and divine approval!

In addition to being the music director of the Rockford Symphony Orchestra in Illinois, Crawford Gates is the music director and conductor of the Beloit-Janesville Symphony Orchestra in Beloit, Wisconsin, and a professor of music and artist-in-residence at Beloit College. He is a commissioned composer whose works include the productions Promised Valley *and* The Hill Cumorah Pageant. *He has served on the MIA General Board and as a member of the Church General Music Committee. Georgia Lauper Gates and he are the parents of four children.*

Emma Lou Thayne

Quest

It was 9:52 A.M., September 28, 1968. I was forty-four years old and walking out of my first class as a graduate student, scared and breathless, but floating. In Orson Spencer Hall I had just tackled a class in Shakespeare's comedies. My teacher was a professor who twenty-nine years before had taught me freshman English and who for nearly twenty of the intervening years had been a sort of colleague as I had spun to the campus between babies and movings to teach freshman English myself—part-time, part-qualified with a B.A., but wholly captivated by those brief encounters with the adult world and learning something beyond a new recipe for left-over little league.

Now I was back as a different person, ablaze with doubt, my long-untested skills as a student on a new line and my long-overextended impulses as a mother, doer of the word, player of the game, in whopping short circuit. Our five children were mostly teenagers, the General Board of the MIA took about forty hours a week, my husband had travel plans, and friends, cabin, courts, lakes, and ski hills held their fascination even as I was propelled over the years into this fearful beginning. I wanted to write—something besides poems for Relief Society and manuals for young people. And I wanted to find out how.

In that first class, young minds had intimidated me even as they had impressed the teacher. I had sat there hearing about Aristotelian unities and thinking, *Somewhere in some dear forgotten past I think I knew something about something like that.*

Now whatever I might once have known blurred in my rusty recall and I sat tight-scalped and prayed, *Dr. Folland, don't call on me for anything—not ever!* What had ever made me think I was ready for any of this? After all, my life was not too bad back there in the kitchen or garden or teaching my M-Men and Gleaners. And seventeen years with preschoolers had allowed me plenty of authenticity in a world I loved and knew I could manage. Why would I have supposed that I could or should be able to come back to school and be anything but an old lady scrambling for her lost youth among the anything-but-lost youth of a new generation?

I took copious notes. I wished I hadn't worn my hose and heels. My stiff hair felt stiff. I knew I would never write a complete sentence or loose a single thought. I sat alone in the middle of disorderly desks and off-handed ableness confused, dejected, ready to run.

Instead, I knew it was time to get up and walk out and pretend I belonged to that awesome font of learning in any but very oblique and ancient fashion. My first workshop, in poetry at 1:10, loomed even more scary than *The Comedy of Errors* ala thirty years later. I picked up my new notebook and my heavy second-hand text, put my stuffed bag on my shoulder, and headed for the library.

Indian Summer warmed the plaza between Orson Spencer and the new Marriott Library. I swung anonymous among the clutches of students, some with the rebellious hair and bra-less composure of the late sixties. How different from us in the forties! But then again, how much the same! Even I, I realized as the sun melted some of my qualms, was that same girl who had gone wide-eyed to Matrology I and sluffed Freshman Orientation before the big war. My heart beat the same, my hands still needed places to finger, surely my head would still function if given even half a green chance. Suddenly I had Fall Fever. The sun lay easy on the bit of arthritis in my shoulders, my feet moved, and the library rose like an entrancing castle across a moat of mud. The campus was in process and so was I.

Inside that library were rows and rows of books, stacks for me to roam in, a new thing called a carrel to study in— a desk with blinders!—and most important, between now and the time anyone would be home from school, I had four huge and beautiful hours that would be uninterrupted. I could play in that library as I had in the canyon in my childhood and with my children in theirs, finding whatever I wanted to, taking my time, trying out a page, relishing, poking about like a pussycat looking for the right spot to settle. I could read, I could write. I soared.

That was the start of a life that would be for me a private excursion into what I had unconsciously—and consciously too, of course—set aside for nearly a quarter of a century, not even knowing I had been only part of myself for all those years.

For the next four quarters I found other parts of me that took wing and flew like fledglings on a June morning. I had workshops in poetry writing, magazine writing, Steinbeck and Chaucer. I wrote papers on Hamlet, Nick Adams, *Dandelion Wine* and the caesura. Many nights my little portable Olivetti and I spent from 11:00 P.M. to 3:00 A.M. spilling out first, second, fifteenth drafts of poems, stories, papers. What I wrote was criticized and praised, honed and cut. Nothing was easy. Nothing was hard. I was dead tired. I loved it.

In the spring of 1970, I marched to the Special Events

Center in a red hood to get my Master of Arts degree in creative writing, tempered by the trembling of the novice who had sat in that first Shakespeare class a year and a half before. By then I had actually learned how to learn. My years of organizing a household or teaching a Mutual class or planning how to put the belongings and temperaments of seven into a station wagon for a week at the beach now fell to moving me toward that degree. I found that with practice and adoration of what I was doing, I could learn to read a book of poems like a novel. I could scan a line of poetry or critique a piece of prose by what was laid by in my graying head filled with calculations for ward tennis tournaments and family bonfires. I could cram for a final or for orals and give it all back on cue just as I'd stayed up all night painting bikes for Christmas or figuring a patio table out of left-over tile from the basement bathroom.

Even more, I had learned something about form and function and even revision. There were ways to make things fit and make sense and always to start over. In school I had the privilege of feeling used in the highest meaning of the word. I found one full measure of my creation. My brain and my soul had made contact. We were off on a whole new life.

As I look back on those months, now over a decade ago, I realize that it was only with the help of people that any of it came about: Friends and counselors who said "Do it." Teachers who said "Work." Advisers who said "This is terrible stuff, try this, do that, read here, there," and finally "*Not bad.*" And there were my family who listened, smiled, were frustrated for me, and happy with me.

With everyone a system had to be worked out. Going to school with a household full of five children under eighteen presents lots of problems. But manageable ones. And sometimes pleasant ones. For instance, on Tuesday nights when their dad taught a class in real estate, the girls and I went for dinner someplace different every week, each girl taking a turn choosing somewhere that we could eat for under a dollar. We'd chat and laugh and come home to watch Mr.

Novak all together and then get on with our studies, all of us sort of compatriots in the game of making do for Wednesday.

In the process my family and I became to each other people, somebodies who shared many of the same worries, many of the same joys. When our older daughter and I met on campus it was like a reunion of old chums. When I hauled thirteen books down to my make-shift study in the storage room, even the littlest came visiting to hear a good poem or read me one of her own. If our meals were less fancy and our bedtimes less predictable, we had marvelous hours late at night when one was in from a date or another had a paper to read and I was still working at the desk Mel had brought home after remodeling his office. He smiled as he paid my tuition or came back to our hotel room at a real estate convention to find me scribbling away or marking up passages that I wanted to read him and then to remember for an essay exam. On the boat at Lake Powell I sat on the bow with pen and pad; in the tent I propped my flashlight under the sleeping bag; under the dryer or on the passenger side of anything, over a kettle or between pulling weeds, school and I carried on a romance that never cooled.

And they came along, my family, my friends, my other occupations, fervid, grinning, sad, boisterous, quiet, frivolous, deep, part of every page.

When I was through, we all knew none of us would ever be through. My going back to school had altered us. We had new ways to care about each other. If as the mother I traded a hobby for a profession, they still participated in that as I did in their most important pursuits. If together we had gleaned from my going to school only new considerations of what the human being is all about, it would have been one of our great religious experiences. But it provided also new appreciation for what the divine in us insisted that we do with our potential.

David Kranes, one of the best teachers I had in that time of great teachers for me, said in a creative writing class that the formula for any creative activity is: genes + store of memory + training. Added to that must be what another mother/writer Pat Capson suggested as essential, especially to those of us who think we're too programmed to let any of the formula congeal as it might, another ingredient—opportunity.

School was that. It mixed the chemicals that turned me out blessed for having been there. For nearly forty-five years I had battled whatever stirred the brew in me that said "Write!" Goodness knows, I had tried to—between other formulas and a thousand thousand insistent inclinations and persuasions. And I had not been unhappy. Only waiting. Until that scary, wonderful day of reentry into the world of teach and learn, where every particle of me was called up for service.

Since then, in long or short moments of struggling to get to the place I am most calm and most excited, my typewriter, I give thanks for whatever gentle construings took me back to the classroom and sent me off filled with wanting to be filled. I have taught new classes, traveled new roads, met new people, tried on old truths in new settings. More than anything, I have found new routes to my own sense of things. My family, my friends, my mountains, my valleys, my God are all closer and more accessible for my having traveled alone to sweet and painful places I could never have discovered on my own.

Emma Lou Warner Thayne is the author of several books of poetry and prose, some of which are Spaces in the Sage, Until Another Day for Butterflies, *and* With Love, Mother. *A new book of essays and poetry,* Alone in New England, *will be published early in 1982. Mrs. Thayne is currently on the* Deseret News *Board of Directors and is a member of the Utah Endowment for the Humanities. She has lectured throughout the United States and enjoys many sports, including skiing, horseback riding and tennis. She is married to Melvin E. Thayne and they have five daughters.*

Larry Chesley

The Lord Doesn't Lie

By the fall of 1976, Annette and I had been married for over three years and still had no children. The Church had been pressing for people to take Lamanite children into their homes and we had friends who had done so, but we did not consider it seriously as a possibility for us. Maybe we were listening to the wrong people, but we'd been led to believe that if you didn't have children of your own it was very difficult to have a Lamanite.

The reasoning made sense: Lamanite children without white "brothers and sisters" felt that the parents were too hard on them, and so they were sometimes resentful; but in families that already had children they could see that the discipline—even if it seemed strict—was fair and that *all* the kids were treated equally. So we had decided that until we had children of our own we would not get into the Lamanite program, and we felt good about our decision. I had, however, told the bishop that if he ever got into a real bind in this matter we would do what we could to help him.

Sure enough, one night Bishop Munk phoned me and said, "Larry, the buses with the Lamanite kids come tomorrow, and we have one boy with no place to stay. We're going to interview a family tonight, and if they take him everything will be fine. But if they don't, would you please consider taking him to live with you?" I felt obligated then to discuss it with Annette, so I kind of teased her a bit about having children in the home, and then we got down to some serious talking about it.

We still had a somewhat negative attitude about it, but we felt that the decision was not really ours alone—we needed to know what the Lord had in mind for us. So we knelt and prayed together to know his will concerning our taking a Lamanite child at that time.

As we prayed, I received what I know to be a revelation in our behalf. The Lord told me that there was a boy who was to come and live in our home, and it was just as sure as anything I've ever known in my life. I told Annette how I felt, and she said she did not have the same strong feeling but, because I have the priesthood and the right to revelation for our family, she was willing to accept my response at face value.

When the bishop called back, as he had said he would, I was very excited. But what he had to say was that the other family had decided to take that boy. This couldn't be right: there was no question in my mind about that revelation to me. So I said, "Bishop, when that family gets tired of that boy, you bring him to us, because . . ." and I explained what had happened to us and asked him to keep it in mind.

When the buses arrived the next day, guess what? There was no Lamanite boy for that other family. Now, this really had me confused, because I knew what the Lord had told me. I let a couple of days go by while I thought about the whole thing and tried to decide what to do. Then I called the

LDS Social Services office. Through working with them on an adoption which had not come through for us, I was familiar with the people there.

I told the brother on the phone that there was an Indian boy who was supposed to be in our home that year, and I asked what I needed to do to go to the reservation to get him. "Sorry," he said, "there's no way. If they don't come on the bus, they can't come. Period."

I told him, "I know that the Lord doesn't lie; I know there is a boy for us." There was a long pause at the other end of the line.

Finally the social worker said, "Brother Chesley, a boy came in on the bus who wasn't supposed to. Maybe he's the one."

Again the bells and the lights and all those wonderful feelings flooded my mind. "Yes," I said, "he's the one!"

"Now, wait a minute! The boy's in a temporary home over on the west side of the valley. They don't have a phone, so I'll have to drive out to ask him if he wants to come and live with you. He wants to go to a big school. He's been living with a family of eight; he may not want to do this, since you don't have any other kids."

"He'll want to come," I said.

And so he came.

His name is Leonard Wheeler. Leonard brought a lot of joy into our life; the year he was with us was a year of growth and blessing for us. He'd been with us for only a couple of months when Annette got pregnant; something we'd been hoping for for a long, long time.

Leonard graduated from high school, but more important than his success at school was that he was a real spiritual giant and a fine example for the rest of his people. Because of him we had many young Lamanites in our home, and we enjoyed them all so much that it really changed our perspective on the program and on the people.

After he finished his year with us, we encouraged Len to go on a mission. But because his mother was dead, he felt he should go back to New Mexico to spend some time with his father. I remember saying to him, "Len, if you leave now, you'll never come back; you'll never go on a mission."

He answered, "Dad, I promise you I'll come back in the fall." He'd never lied to us; I had no reason to question him now. So he left us that summer and went home to earn a little money, but he was back in the fall to send in the paper work and prepare himself to go on a mission. And the Lord called him to teach his own—the Navajo people of the Holbrook Arizona Mission. We were happy to support him on that mission; he served honorably for two years and then returned to our home.

Leonard went away a boy, as all missionaries do, and he came back a man—strong in the gospel, knowledgeable in the gospel. He has the ability to be a great leader of his own people. He went back on the reservation to work in a hardware store. He's done something many of the Lamanites in the placement program don't do: he's returned to his people to help them improve themselves and especially to help them increase spiritually.

Leonard Wheeler is a great boy, a great man, a son of God. He knows that, and we know it, too. He brought great happiness into our home, and we are grateful for the privilege of having him.

After graduating from high school, Lt. Col. Larry Chesley served four years in the United States Air Force in Japan and Germany. Later he graduated from Weber State College, then rejoined the Air Force and was assigned a tour of duty in Vietnam. There he was shot down and held as a prisoner of war for nearly seven years. His book, Seven Years in Hanoi, *tells of his experiences. He and his wife, Annette Huntsman Chesley, have six children.*

Victor L. Brown, Jr.

Fathers and Fathering

A very tense woman sat in my office seeking professional treatment for anxieties about her forthcoming marriage. She had divorced her first husband and now feared that the same problems would doom the second marriage even before it began. I had difficulty understanding her at first because it appeared to me that she had little reason to fear anything. She was unusually well-educated, attractive, and obviously intelligent.

As I pressed her as to why she was anxious about this marriage she finally exclaimed, "My father doesn't love me and he never has!" Then she sobbed as if her whole heart were breaking. This woman was so hurt by her relationship with her father that she could not develop one with a husband.

Several years passed after that interview during which I gave no special thought to it. Then one day, after a particularly challenging interview, I was struck by a trait that seemed to exist in the personal histories of many of my recent clients: almost all of them had troubled relationships with their fathers. I then asked some of my colleagues if this applied to their clients as well. After reviewing their cases, they agreed. It was then I remembered that woman from years gone by and, as a result of all these experiences, a principle was established which has become a cornerstone of my professional, religious and personal understanding.

The principle is that the eternal title and role of *father* is profoundly and irreplaceably important to every one of us — so important, in fact, that I have come to believe that to prevent or diagnose emotional disturbance, one of the key factors to examine is the person's relationship with his or her father.

Motherhood is so powerful that its brilliance has tended to obscure the less obvious but equally critical power of fatherhood. Perhaps motherhood is like the sun, warming all creation with widespread rays, while fatherhood is like a laser beam, focused and intense.

Over the years I have studied fathers. One was a very busy stake president. He held a major government position, served as a Boy Scout official, and practiced a demanding profession. He and his wife were the parents of ten children. I once asked his wife how he could possibly be an effective husband and father. She replied rather firmly, "When my husband is home, he is *really home!*"

As time passed I came to know this man as a dear friend, and I discovered that he had a trait that at first upset me. We would occasionally take our children out on holidays to play ball, and on those outings whenever I tried to bring up Church or professional matters that were on my mind he would very abruptly cut me off. This offended me until I finally realized that he was doing precisely what his wise wife had said: when he was with his children, he was really *with* them and not thinking about the office or the stake.

Another father I know very well has enjoyed unusual professional success, actually worldwide esteem. Yet to me his highest achievement has been the reordering of priorities. One evening he failed to come into the office after dinner, as had been his habit for years. The next day he explained that while he knew he had an important report to finish, his son had wanted help building a doghouse. From that point on I have seen this father consistently and earnestly place his wife and children at the top of his priority list.

This matter has been more than emotions and stories for me. I have scrutinized research data and used this in my clinical work. The evidence is there. Fathering is a factor which influences mental and spiritual well-being for good or ill.

A daughter's self-esteem and school performance are affected by her relationship with her father. A son's choice of professional and religious activity is an extension of fatherly influence. Research data show these patterns. My clinical experience shows it. The gospel teaches it with eternal solemnity.

The attention and genuine interest of a father to his family literally create a coat of armor in combatting the emotional stress of our time. Inattention and disinterest lead to tragic weakness.

One man I know has dreams in which he yearns for his father's physical touch: any kind of touch—an embrace, a hit, a wrestle, a handshake. In his thirty years of life he cannot recall his father's touching him with any emotional meaning. Another man had the healing experience of seeing his father completely rearrange his priorities for the family.

I have wondered why fathers are so important. Mothers are irreplaceable for very obvious reasons and thank heaven, most of them are true to their eternal role. But fathers perhaps make the difference between ordinary and extraordinary family well-being. I believe that fathers largely form their children's beliefs in God, the Heavenly Father. One man told me he could not pray with confidence, and in the course of treatment we found that God to him was like his earthly father, angry and not really interested.

When fathers are missing, the Church provides ways to

compensate. President Joseph F. Smith, son of the martyr Hyrum, was raised by his widowed mother, clearly a remarkable woman. Even so, he had "foster" fathers such as Brigham Young, Heber C. Kimball, and his bishop — all of whom guided and loved him.

I know a man who has been foster father to many boys and girls besides his own children. He and his wife have practiced pure religion by giving time, money, and love to children needing fathers. They have offered employment, work on the stake welfare farm and, in many cases, a place in their home and family. From this man I have come to believe that there ought not to be one "orphan" in The Church of Jesus Christ of Latter-day Saints.

I worry when I see friends and colleagues submerged in vocational, Church and personal activities while other men try to substitute for them at home. I yearn for the day when nurturant fatherhood — not wealth, not professional status, not athletics, not even Church position — is counted as true success.

I must confess that this knowledge about fathers and fathering has not always been comfortable. Personally and professionally, it has provoked me to discard many ideas which I used to value highly. No longer can I justify evenings or weekends away from home on professional or Church assignments. Certain hobbies have had to change. The net result, though, has been some very special joys through improved relations with my family. Through all this, my regard for my wife — who held things together at our home all by herself for our first seventeen years — approaches reverence as I consider how she compensated for my neglect. I hope to live long and well enough to honor her and my children sufficiently for their love and patience.

Victor L. Brown, Jr., has been the director of the Brigham Young University Comprehensive Clinic and the Institute for Studies in Values and Human Behavior. He is currently the Northern California Area Director of Church Welfare Services, an adjunct professor at BYU, and a stake high councilor. He has written a book, Human Intimacy, *which will be published in 1982. He is married to Mareen Holdaway Brown and they have six children.*

George Romney

A Matchless
Promise

Our lives are shaped by the ideas that we treasure. Shortly after I had married my high school sweetheart, we went to visit a slightly older couple whom we both admired. The husband had been my wife's Sunday School teacher, and I had looked up to him as a returned missionary, a former college football star and, at the time of our visit, the western hand of a great American financial institution.

In discussing my future vocational plans, he said to me, "Never be afraid to make a break." It was an idea nugget that I placed in my brain's permanent retention vault.

At the time I was employed as an apprentice at the Aluminum Company of America, the nation's only producer of aluminums. Shortly after that experience I was transferred from Alcoa's Los Angeles office to its Washington, D.C., office. We were thrilled to be working in Washington and very happy with my new responsibilities. They enabled us to

form friendships with many interesting and influential individuals in government as well as those representing private
economic organizations.

Within eight years we had become the delighted parents
of two little girls and had moved into a beautiful new home
built to our specifications. My future with Alcoa was assured:
I had complete security for life and the opportunity to grad-
ually move up the corporate ladder. We loved Washington,
we loved our friends, we loved life there.

One of our friends there represented the Automobile
Manufacturers Association, and in 1939 he was made president of it. This was the trade association whose members
included all the companies manufacturing cars and trucks.
The heads of the motor vehicle companies directed him to
remain in Washington and to employ someone else to
manage the Association's main office in Detroit. He offered
me that job.

Now, a trade association does not offer the job security
and advancement opportunity of a major corporation—
particularly one like Alcoa was then. My wife and I faced a
difficult decision. Should we leave beautiful, exciting Washington for industrial Detroit? Should we give up Alcoa
security and opportunity for an uncertain future in the trade
association of the highly competitive automobile industry?
Should we leave our cherished friends and sacrifice our
brand new home?

To make the right decision we followed the Lord's formula, which is the only way to be certain you have the right
answer. It is found in Doctrine and Covenants 90:24 and
consists of three steps: search diligently, pray always, and be
believing. We searched diligently. I went to Detroit and
talked with the car company presidents. I talked with
knowledgeable government officials and friends, some of
whom discouraged us from accepting. They said, "You'll
never be successful in the automobile industry. The car
company executives are cigar-chewing, whiskey-drinking,
tough men." But after "searching diligently" and much
praying, we received the definite answer—we should go to

Detroit. We believed, and we made the break, moving to Michigan in 1940.

There was no way we could foresee how this would enrich our lives beyond anything that could have happened with Alcoa. Within two years I was managing the greatest voluntary industrial wartime cooperative effort in history as managing director of the Automotive Council for War Production. The Council members included not only the motor vehicle companies but also the parts-producing companies, body companies, rubber companies, and tool and die companies. These companies produced over 25 percent of all the metal armaments America used and supplied in World War II, and their cooperative efforts speeded their volume production enough to shorten World War II by at least seven months.

This experience was followed by further reliance on the Lord's formula and the faith it provided to make further breaks which in turn resulted in unforeseeable experiences, both private and public: selling the first successful small car in America (the Rambler), leading a citizen effort that secured a new state constitution, serving three terms as governor, and later holding a position in the President's cabinet. And all this was because Michigan was the place for us.

However, the richest experience was participating in the growth of the Church in Michigan. In 1940 there were only a few small branches. In 1952 the first Michigan stake was organized. Today there are nine stakes within the boundaries of that original stake.

The Lord's decision-making formula (D&C 90:24) concludes with a matchless promise: "Search diligently, pray always, and be believing, and all things shall work together for your good, if ye walk uprightly and remember the covenant wherewith ye have covenanted one with another."

Formerly president, chairman of the board and general manager of American Motors Corporation, George W. Romney is now national chairman of Volunteer: National Center for Citizen Involvement. From

1963 to 1969 he served as governor of the state of Michigan, then resigned to become the Secretary of the Department of Housing and Urban Development. He completed a mission to Scotland and England as a young man and has served in many Church callings including that of Regional Representative.

Linda Eyre

A Joyful
Mother
of Children

I could feel it coming on. The baby was getting around on his own pretty well, and I felt wonderful. The other four children, although they had their individual ups and downs, were basically secure and happy. The piano practicing was getting more regular because I was able to be behind it a little more consistently. And with the baby just beginning to walk, I felt wings of independence and a sense of joy in watching the children grow and relate to the world around them. What worried me was just the nagging feeling in the back of my mind that it might be time to have another baby.

I quickly remembered the many times I had said to myself when the last baby was tiny, *Now remember, remember, remember how hard it is to have a new little baby! It takes all your time and attention. You never get enough sleep because you're up twice in the night with the baby, and then of course there's no hope for a nap during the day with a two-year-old and a four-year-old in the house, both ready to "search and destroy" at any moment. You're so tired that you're a grouch with your husband and children all the time. Besides, you have to be on duty every three or four hours to nurse the baby—day and night—so that every outing, whether it be a fireside or grocery shopping, has to be scheduled to the minute. Waking every morning to the baby's cries cuts down on and sometimes eliminates your time with the scriptures and makes it much harder to have morning prayer. And it's like a bell ringing to start the morning's never-ending race to change and feed the baby while you supervise the practicing and settle an argument about who gets to sit by Daddy before organizing the break-fast amidst pleas of "write my teacher a note" and "give me some lunch money." Then you get to dress and then redress the two-year-old who has been using the butter for play-dough while you check to see that the beds are made and oversee the getting ready for school, complete with the perpetual last-minute scramble for Saren's toothbrush, Shawni's mittens and Josh's shoes. Finally you struggle to get them out of the door with a pasted smile over your gritted teeth and a "have a nice day." Next you try to help Saydi get her shirt on frontwards for nursery school while talking on the phone to someone with a problem, and then you have to fish the cat out of the toilet where Saydi has put him to "try his luck." You just don't have time for another baby!* I told myself over and over to remember how lovely the comparative peace of routine was becoming.

We, as a family, were just going into the third year of the greatest opportunity of our lives. My husband was president of the London South Mission, and we were having a mar-velous experience—not without challenges, however, as the demands were great. Feeding mobs of missionaries, speaking at conferences, preparing our home for firesides for investi-gators and for new members who were struggling, and fixing dinners for everyone from stake presidents to General Authorities to members of Parliament kept me hopping.

Always before I had been thoroughly excited about the

prospect of having a new spirit join our family. We had been
married eight years and had five children: Saren, 7; Shawni,
6; Josh, 4; and Saydi, 2½ had come with us from America,
and we had been blessed to have one child born in England
—our little British boy, Jonah. My hesitation this time caused
me to examine my own heart. Was I afraid after Jonah's
difficult arrival? That was not it. Could it be that I simply did
not want to give up my freedom to participate in all the
activities of the mission? As I wrestled with the pros and
cons (mostly cons) and with the deep, dark feeling I got
every time I thought about another baby, my husband, who
was feeling the same dilemma, suggested that on Sunday we
should follow the same procedure that we had with the
other children and have a special day of fasting and prayer to
get "an answer."

To be very honest, I did not even want to ask, because I
was afraid of what the answer might be. However, I finally
consented, with the thought in mind that maybe the answer
this time *might* be "No, not yet, take care of the responsibilities you have now and wait." *Oh, please tell me that!* I
thought.

"Okay, Richard," I said in my most determined voice.
"But we have *got* to have a very explicit answer and we'll
have to fast forty-eight or even seventy-two hours, if necessary, to be absolutely sure!" I saw him go a little pale around
the mouth, because fasting is one of his *hardest* things. After
a minute he patted me on the shoulder and said, "Let's start
with twenty-four and see how it goes."

Sunday rolled around, and as we neared the end of our
fast we compared our lists of pros and cons and started
talking about it in earnest so that we could take a *yes* or *no*
decision to the Lord for confirmation. About that time,
however, the children began to get pretty noisy and Daddy
called Saren, our oldest, over to the table.

"Would you please take your brothers and sisters up to
the playroom and entertain them for an hour while Mom and
Dad have a very serious talk, honey?" Curious about what
we were doing, our very mature little seven-year-old de-

manded to know what was so important before she would consent.

"Well," he said after a moment of deliberation, "we're trying to decide whether or not to ask Heavenly Father to send a new little person to be in our family." She smiled wryly and happily herded the others up the stairs.

For what seemed like a very long time, we worked on an extensive list of possibilities and finally decided mutually much to my chagrin that it was the right time to have another baby if we could get a confirmation from the Lord and if he would grant us that privilege once again. As we knelt down, I remember feeling what I can only describe as *black*, dark and numb. I just didn't know how I could possibly do it! I suppose I was hoping not for a confirmation but for a "stupor of thought" that would tell us to reconsider.

Kneeling across from me and holding my hands, Richard began the prayer. The minute he said, "We have decided that now is the time to ask for another choice spirit, if that is thy will for us," I began to feel what I would describe as a bright light of peace settling over me, starting from the top of my head and spreading to every part, right down to my fingers and toes. It was as though the Lord was saying *forcefully,* in his own peaceful way, "It's all right Linda. This baby is what you need; I've got a good one up here—one who needs to come *now* and who will teach you many things. I'll provide a way to get it all done. All is well. Be at peace."

By the time the prayer was finished and I had offered mine, a conviction that a new person would soon join us and that all *would* be well was burning inside me, overwhelmingly, all-consuming and undeniable. I was a new person, at perfect peace and ready for change. Most answers the Lord had given me were not nearly so dramatic—only nudges in the right direction and good feelings. I was so gratified for this special, *sure* knowledge that he was there, loving and caring and answering.

While we were still holding hands and glowing in the aftermath of this beautiful spiritual experience, Saren, who could somehow sense that we were finished, came trotting into the dining room with a happy smile on her face and some pieces of paper in her hand.

"I organized the kids upstairs," she said. "I had them all sit in a circle on the floor and gave them each a piece of paper. Shawni and I wrote the names of the kids at the top of each paper. We told them to put a big check in the middle of the paper if they wanted a new baby brother or sister." She handed me five pieces of paper with five bold checkmarks below the names. It was now a unanimous *family* decision!

In the following few days, largely because of the good feelings I had about the answer the Lord had given me, I felt particularly close to him and my mind was flooded with things that were revelations to me. I had been going along these past seven years being a faithful Mormon mother—having children, and learning the "hows" and "whens" and "wheres" but without really realizing the "*whys*"!

I projected myself ahead in time and tried to look at life and the child-bearing years from an eternal perspective. I was startled to realize that in all eternity I have only about twenty years in which to bear physical children on a physical earth and reap the eternal joys therein—the joy of learning to manage time and feelings and people, and the joy of molding lives and developing relationships which will help me to learn and grow forever. Only twenty years! Right now it seems like such a *long* time to change diapers and stand in foyers with fussy, noisy children, to prepare meals and put on bandages. Yet (as so many mothers just past the child-bearing years tell me), so soon there will be only a memory of how I did, to what extent I was anxiously engaged in grasping all the joy and happiness that was there for me to find in that short time. Then it is over—forever!

I began to concentrate less on the difficulties of pregnancy and child-bearing, on the complications of organizing life around an infant, on the heavy responsibility of another person totally dependent on me. I began to see it all from a new perspective: my eyes were opened, and like a warm, wooly parachute settling over me, I began to discover the "whys."

Having another child is a great blessing to be looked forward to with enthusiasm and excitement. I began to relish the change (the essence of the Savior's message: "You can change") and the challenges that follow, to pour my energies into our real priority and to organize my life to do so, because that opportunity for that particular time in life only comes once and doesn't last very long. Children grow and change; so do situations; so do I. I began to relish the joy of balancing my life to make scrubbing floors and windows secondary and watching and relating to children, perceiving their needs before they became real problems, first.

I began to realize what a great blessing it is to struggle to teach a child the correct principles of life and to make our home a great medium to do so. What we teach our children, how we mold their characters to try to make them responsible family members, loyal citizens, and noble children of God, affects not only us and them but their children and their children's children—an awesome and exciting challenge!

As the days passed I began to realize that my body was my most valuable earthly possession because of the miracles it could perform. If the condition that it was in was the determining factor in how many children I'd be privileged to have, I'd better take it a little more seriously. I felt an urgency to get in first-class physical condition so that I would be *able* to bear children as well as humanly possible for me. I decided that being in shape would alleviate the discomfort of the first few and last few months of the pregnancy, not to mention the benefits to the health of the baby. I had always known it made a difference, but I hadn't taken it seriously enough in the past to worry much about it. By "number six" with the hopes of more to come, it was serious business. I began a short crash course of physical fitness and realized that keeping fit between pregnancies was as important as during. The whole revelation was exhilarating.

The things that had worried me during past pregnancies seemed small and unimportant in light of the eternal perspective. Suddenly all the counsel given by the prophets came to life: "Have children unless there are health reasons involved. Put your family first; cut out the trivia, the excess, and concentrate on *them*. The rewards will be immediate *and* long-term . . . forever."

Those were the feelings that came to me in England. And our sixth child was even more of a blessing than the Lord had promised us. But that was months ago. How is it going today?

I often reflect on an experience which reconfirmed my feelings. I had to get to a certain department store to return two big bedspreads which I had taken for my Mom to approve. Deciding that I would just have time to get them returned and still pick up my two oldest children at school within half an hour, I piled the other four in the car (one of them without shoes, as it was midsummer and I simply didn't have any more time to search).

In the store I discovered that there was no elevator, so I quickly organized a "plan for the escalator." Because they would not allow open strollers on the moving stairs, I folded mine up and hung it over my right arm. On the same arm I perched that sweet sixth baby—now a seven-month-old angel innocently sucking his fist and completely unaware of my dilemma.

In my left hand I had the large plastic garbage sack into which I had put the bedspreads to protect them from the peanut butter. In front of me were five-year-old Josh, studying the mechanics of the escalator, and two-year-old Jonah, fidgeting around with no shoes on his feet. Behind me was cute four-year-old Saydi in her self-chosen "orphan outfit," wearing jam from ear to ear, singing embarrassingly loud (thus destroying my efforts to remain unnoticed) and enjoying the ride.

As we approached the top, Josh got off with a grand gesture of accomplishment, but Jonah, bless his screeching little heart, panicked and bolted, deciding he was *not* getting off and was going back down. The scene that resulted was hysterical. Josh started yelling, "Hey, Mom, Jonah's *stuck!*" Jonah started screaming at the top of his lungs. I grabbed for him, thinking surely his little toes were being mangled in the "iron teeth," and Saydi, who was helplessly being bashed into me from behind and was "bellering" like a sick cow. Poor baby Talmadge was screaming with horror because, as I had lurched to grab Jonah, he had fallen backwards and was literally hanging upside down by his knees on my arm.

Somehow I got everybody off that escalator with no fatalities, and I comforted the snuffly children and dried their tears. Completely hassled and upset at myself for being so stupid as to even *try* such a dumb thing, all I could think of was, "Linda, what are you *doing* with all these *kids!*"

I quickly tried to compose myself and hurry on, as I knew that my two grade-schoolers would be waiting. As luck would have it, I got behind two very slow little old ladies— one in rubber boots and the other in a little black pillbox hat with net flowing around the top. We were in a narrow aisle and simply could *not* get past. They had been near the "scene of the accident," but even though there were still some whimpers and sniffles, they were completely oblivious to my situation.

Just at the point of exasperation, I couldn't help hearing one say to the other in a very loud but sweet little-old-lady voice (I'm not sure which one was hard of hearing), "Oh, no, Agnes, I don't want any yarn today; I've got enough yarn to last for two years!"

That statement really sunk in, and I stopped dead in my tracks and started to giggle about the whole situation. As I looked at those two little ladies picking through the yarn and then glanced back at my whimpering children, I got a flash of inspiration as the answer to my question. A feeling of sheer joy and gratitude for my children overwhelmed me. I *knew* what I was doing with all these kids, and I was *so* happy to be in my shoes instead of in the other ladies' "boots."

Inevitably we all get into some "dire" situations at times, and for my part I find it helps to lighten the load if I can look at them with a little humor, as I was able to on this occasion. This helps me to put things in perspective too, and particularly to reinforce my sense of appreciation.

I hope no one will misunderstand what I have written here. I am certainly not advocating that all parents should have lots of children. I am merely trying to share the exhilarating feeling of knowing that as wives and mothers, husbands and fathers, we are entitled to personal revelation, especially when it concerns our own or our children's lives and what has been foreordained for them. This is true whether our children number one or ten, and whether the Lord sends them to us through natural means or adoption. This is a glorious knowledge.

When times are hard (and certainly there are times of real trial, not just momentary desperation), I remember that sure, sweet answer that my Heavenly Father gave me that assured us we were to have that sixth child. It scares me to think of the resentments and doubts I might have felt if I had just gone ahead with having new babies without that calm, peaceful assurance from the Lord.

The child-bearing years are without doubt the most frustrating, demanding, physically and emotionally trying times of a woman's life. But those hard times, filled with the mistakes and purifying experiences necessary to help us grow, are the finest part of life. They constitute one of life's greatest challenges — to become, as Psalm 113:9 puts it, "a *joyful mother of children.*"

Linda Jacobson Eyre is a musician, teacher, and writer. She was born in Montpelier, Idaho, and was raised on a farm. She attended Utah State University, where she graduated with honors in Music Education. Later she taught music in the Boston, Massachusetts, public schools. From 1976 to 1979 she and her husband were called to preside over the London South Mission of the Church. In 1981 she was named the Young Mother of the Year from Utah. She is the co-author of the book Teaching Children Joy. *She and her husband, Richard, have homes in Salt Lake City, Utah, and McLean, Virginia. They are the parents of seven children.*